HOME-MADE

First published 1983

by Search Press Ltd.,
Wellwood, North Farm Road,
Tunbridge Wells, Kent. TN2 3DR

in conjunction with

Sterling Publishing Co. Inc.,
2 Park Avenue,
New York, NY 10016, U.S.A.

Home-Made and at a fraction of the cost is based upon and expanded from the individual paperback volumes of the *Home-Made* series, published and not yet published, with text and drawings by Polly Pinder and the text from *Smoked Foods* by Richard Pinney. The published titles are *Breads, Drinks, Herbs in Pots, Soaps, Smoked Foods, Scents and Fragrances, Cosmetics,* and *Soft Cheeses;* all copyright © Search Press Ltd 1978.

The author and the publishers gratefully acknowledge Richard Pinney's text for *Smoked Foods* as the basis for Chapter 5 of the present book.

ISBN (UK)   0 85532 530 5

Printed in Italy by L. E. G. O. Vicenza

HOME-MADE

and at a fraction of the cost

POLLY PINDER

SEARCH PRESS LTD
in association with
STERLING PUBLISHING CO. INC.

Contents

Growing herbs in pots 8

It is fascinating to watch the growth of different fragrant plants as they develop from tiny seedlings

Home-baked breads 20

Once you have baked and eaten your own bread, you will never be satisfied with a shop-bought loaf.

Soft cheeses 36

Making cheese at home is as simple as making bread — you do not need a cow in the back garden!

Chutneys, pickles and mustards 46

It makes sense to have a pickling session when there is a glut of cheap fruit and vegetables.

Smoked foods 56

A complete system of smoke curing — the salting, smoke drying and cooking—without a smokehouse.

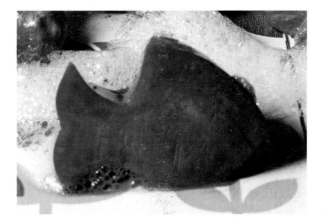

Introduction

We seem to have a deep-rooted need to make things. This may be connected, in some way, with the fact that our early ancestors made, from necessity, their own things — tools, clothes, even their own dwellings. As man evolved, so did the community, and certain members chose to specialize in making and providing specific requirements and services for their community. As this developed over the centuries, people, particularly in the more densely populated areas, tended to lose the necessity, desire and capability of providing their requirements through their own creative work. Country folk, however, seem to have retained that ability, no doubt because of their isolation and their closeness to the land — being more aware of the provisions which nature bestows on those who take the time and trouble to search out and utilise her gifts.

Over the last few decades — expense probably being a major factor — people appear to have become keenly interested in creative activities: the book market has been flooded with manuals on repairs and maintenance, do-it-yourself, carpentry, rug-making and even (back to our ancient ancestors) designing and building their own houses, using man's increased technology to adapt nature's resources.

This, coupled with a revived interest and concern in the more basic and natural foods, has led to an upsurge in the awareness of people's own capabilities — we *can* look after and make things for ourselves, we do not *always* have to ask the assistance and services of other members of our community.

This is not a fanatical do-it-yourself book. It does not declare emphatically that a 'home-made, brown, whole-wheat loaf' is better than a 'pre-sliced, white loaf' (even though it is!) or that home-made soap is superior to commercial soap. Who can deny that there is a place for all of these things in our lives? And where children are concerned — mine, who genuinely prefer home-made bread and home-made jam for their tea, will give shouts and whoopees if I suggest a white sliced loaf when my stock of bread has been demolished. Simply because it is rare, they seem to like a change, as do we all.

. . . So do not decry the fish finger, the saucy baked bean, the factory-made nylon rug or the identical skirts which dangle on the hangers of boutiques — they all have their place, and we need them; *but*, there is such an enormous amount of pleasure and satisfaction to be gained from doing and making things for ourselves that the terms 'home-made' and 'hand-made' can never be lightly dismissed; they imply a certain care, a love which has gone into the making of something rather special.

How do we react when we are given a birthday card by a child who has spent hours drawing and colouring the flowers, people and odd little details? The card usually takes pride of place, in the forefront of all the other cards, because it was made for us with love. And that applies to everything which is 'home-made' be it a

goat's milk cheese

vanilla fudge

pot of jam, a pair of bedroom curtains, a slightly slanting shelf, everything — even if, while you are still hot and flushed baking the bread, the children throw a ball and break the kitchen window. Even then, the love is still there; the pleasure of giving is not diminished, and the pleasure of eating is not diminished. Therefore, to make things for yourself, your family, and friends is a good and noble occupation.

This book could not possibly attempt to encourage all spheres of the home-made arts. One has to specialize a little, so most of the topics treated here are based in and around the kitchen, the heart of the home, using as many natural ingredients as possible.

There are some chapters on the more usual kitchen occupations: bread, preserve and sweet making, for example (but these include interesting and unusual recipes); and there are other chapters on less common subjects; cheeses, smoked foods, cosmetics and soaps.

Together they all provide an exciting challenge, with the additional satisfaction of knowing that you have: baked a delicious tomato and oregano loaf; smoked some herring; produced your own pot-pourri; made some goat's milk cheese or created an exotic cream perfume — all by yourself.

As with all things these days, the question of expense has to be considered, particularly when one is living on a fixed income, as many people are. Without a doubt, it is cheaper to make something yourself than to buy it. But how much cheaper will depend on how well your project is planned. To buy a large amount of an unusual ingredient, when you will be using only a quarter of that amount, is adding to, rather than reducing the expense. Good planning cannot be over-emphasized. Similar to the supermarket concept of bulk buying, usually the more you make of something, the cheaper it becomes — and this is where one of man's recent boons comes to the fore — the freezer. But of course, not everything has to be frozen: many recipes have their own preserving properties, for example, jams, pickles and smoked foods.

In short, the most economical way of making anything is to plan beforehand: exactly which ingredients or items are required; whether, if there is anything left, you will be able to use it in another recipe; and whether you can practically store large amounts of the finished product.

Finally, a word of warning for all of you who have children. Some of the subjects covered in this book are suitable for children to become involved with: the early stages of bread-making; certain stages of the sweet-making process; hulling the strawberries; or planting herb seeds. But others are most definitely not — a pan of boiling preserve can give the most horrific scalding, as can caustic soda (one of the main ingredients of soap-making). So please be careful. Read the introduction to each chapter and decide whether or not the children should be around, before you actually start any of the recipes.

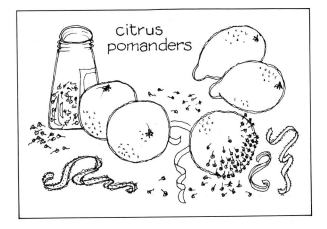
citrus pomanders

spiced egg soap

Growing herbs in pots

Introduction

Growing herbs in pots is a splendid occupation for lazy gardeners — or for anyone with either a small garden or none at all. Many fresh herbs are never available in shops and packets of dried herbs are a poor substitute; the alternative is to grow your own.

When I started growing herbs and had read many books on the subject, I became increasingly confused by information and advice given on the various feeds and composts to be used. Eventually I decided to use a seed compost for the seeds, a potting compost for the plants and mix the two if I was short of one.

Basic guidelines are given here for growing all the herbs in this chapter. More specific information is given under each herb heading.

What is a herb?

Generally a herb is a fragrant plant with a soft stem whose flowers, seeds, leaves, stems and roots can be used (without prior drying) for the flavouring of dishes or for medicinal purposes.

The distinction between a herb and a spice is small. Some cookery experts refer to all herbs which are used for seasoning, as spices; sometimes the naturally hard parts of the herb — roots and seeds — are called spices.

Spices, the *dried* flowers, seeds, leaves, roots or bark of aromatic plants give a much stronger and more piquant flavour when added to dishes. They can also be used as preservatives.

Having said that, this chapter is concerned with the growing of several fragrant plants for culinary or medicinal use — but mainly for pleasure.

A concise herbal history

One of the earliest herbals is believed to have been written in China over 2,500 years BC. At about the same time herbs were being used in India, Assyria and Egypt as remedies for many diverse ailments.

The ancient Greeks also used herbs for medicinal purposes. Hippocrates, the 'Father of Medicine', born in 477 BC, had extensive botanical knowledge. Among his prescriptions was the use of garlic and rue to relieve childbirth pains.

When the Romans occupied Britain in 43 AD, they brought with them the seeds of many different herbs which had been imported from their Mediterranean colonies. Of these garlic was held in high esteem, being issued daily to the labourers and soldiers as a strengthening medicine. It was also used as an efficient antiseptic for wounds and sores.

During the 'dark ages' in Europe the cultivation of herbs seems to have almost died out, except among the scattered communities of monks who still maintained their monastery herb gardens. This was eventually changed through the expansion of the Muslim Empire and the consequent Crusades. The Persian physician, Avicenna (980–1037), discovered the method of extracting the volatile oils of herbs by distillation.

As trade between East and West increased so did the exportation of herbs and spices to Northern Europe. Herbals, which had been written and re-copied in manuscript form by generations of monks and which were often beautifully illuminated with botanical drawings, gained a wider public with the invention of printing. The first printed herbals (fifteenth century) were illustrated with charming stylized woodcuts, which became more naturalistic as the science of botany developed.

Herbs were now becoming an integral part of the lives of both peasant and lord. They were used not only as culinary and medicinal aids, but also for the making of herbal beers and wines, cosmetics and insect repellents, and generally to sweeten the air in otherwise rather fetid dwellings. John Gerard, a gentleman of London (1545–1612), spent most of his life growing plants and writing about them. In *The Herbal or General History of Plants*, published in 1597, he described the cultivation of many of the new species of herbs which had been brought back from North and South America by the seafaring explorers of his time.

During the sixteenth and seventeenth centuries the transmission of seeds and roots between Europe and the Americas increased. Settlers in the 'New World' sent specimens to various herb centres in Europe; while new colonists were requested to bring European seeds to America.

Nicholas Culpeper (1616–1654) whose *Complete Herbal and English Physician* was both popular and

Sweet Marjoram with tiny knotted flowers. See page 12

controversial, is still widely read. His book caused controversy among contemporary professionals because in it he questioned the integrity of the physicians and insulted the herbalists and botanists by linking the medicinal properties of herbs with the study of astrology.

In this century two world wars have increased the popular interest in herbs (because of inadequate and uninteresting diets); as did *A Modern Herbal* written by Mrs Grieve and published in 1931.

Today, the tremendous upsurge of interest shown in herbalism can be judged by the number of books available on the subject. The culinary, dietary, medicinal and cosmetic value of herbs cannot be disputed; nor can the joy and satisfaction obtained by actually growing them yourself.

Cultivation

You can buy herb seed packets from most nurserymen, and there are specialist suppliers in most counties, whose addresses can be obtained from directories.

As you will probably want at the most six pots of each herb, seed trays are unnecessary. Disposable plastic coffee cups are ideal for seeds, or you can also use yoghurt cartons. Wash the cups and cut a drainage

hole in the bottom of each. Using a good seed compost (it should be moist), fill to within ½in. (1.25 cm) of the top. Put four seeds, slightly apart, in each cup and sprinkle with a little more compost. Arrange the cups on a tray and slide this into a large plastic bag. Carefully transfer everything to a dark place.

Inspect the cups each morning and evening. As soon as the seedlings appear, remove the cups from the bag. Place them on a windowsill facing south, east or west.

Transplant the seedlings to a larger pot when the first two seed-leaves are fully formed, but before the true leaves appear. Choose the healthiest seedlings (not those with very long, straggly stems). Fill the bottom of the plant pot with a few pebbles and some coarse sand (if it is available). Use a good brand of potting compost. The compost should be moist, never bone-dry or soaking wet.

Here is a check list of necessary equipment: packets of seeds; seed compost; potting compost; small pebbles for drainage; disposable plastic coffee cups or yoghurt cartons; adhesive labels to identify seeds; plant pots (unglazed clay pots have a slight advantage over plastic ones because the porous walls will allow excess water to evaporate, thus preventing the plant from becoming waterlogged — but with careful watering this will not happen); an old dessert spoon; a hand water spray.

General care

Most herbs originate from the warmer climates of the world and are not used to frequent rainfall. Never over-water your herbs, as the pot will become water-logged and this quickly leads to rotting roots and the consequent death of the plant. When the compost feels dry round the edge of the pot, water the plant. Use rain water if possible, if not use tepid water from the tap.

Herbs are at their best just before the plant comes into flower. Pick the leaves from the top of the plant and remove any which are yellow.

Allow your herbs some fresh air occasionally (but never put them in a direct draught) and spray them at intervals with tepid water — you can buy a small hand water-spray from nurserymen and garden centres.

In order to keep your herbs bushy and compact, it is necessary to trim them back in the summer. Pinch out all the centre shoots and also cut off any straggly runners as near to the base as possible.

Your herbs will also need feeding during the summer months. Use a good brand of liquid bio food. Only a few drops are required (read the manufacturer's instructions) and are added to the water before watering. Never put undiluted feed straight into the pot.

Check the underneath of the pot regularly. If root fibre is beginning to grow from the drainage hole, the plant needs transferring to a larger pot — so tap the sides of the pot, turn it upside down and carefully ease out the plant and as much of the root-ball as possible. Re-pot, not forgetting to put pebbles and sand into the new pot first. After adding some extra compost, firm it down, then water and feed the plant.

You will enjoy growing herbs and using them to bring variety to your culinary dishes. It is also fascinating to watch the growth of the different fragrant plants.

Parsley

Parsley is my favourite herb. The sweet tangy flavour bursts out as it touches the taste buds. Wonderful!

There are several varieties of parsley. All are biennial and can grow to 12in. (60cm) high. The plants have bright green foliage and produce small yellow-green flowers in the second year. The curled moss variety (the young plants opposite) has deeply divided, curly leaves; the fern leaf variety has small flat leaves.

Cultivation

Read the notes on cultivation and general care, pages 9–10. Germination of parsley seeds takes rather longer than most — sometimes as long as 2 months. It is possible to hasten the process slightly by steeping the seeds overnight in warm water, just before sowing. When the seedlings produce their first two leaves they can be transplanted in the normal way or put into a 'parsley pot' — these can be bought from most garden centres. Put two or three seedlings in each hole. Parsley loves the sun, so if possible, place your pot on a south facing windowsill. When the plant is in its second year all the flower stalks should be cut off to prevent seeding. The foliage should be picked frequently to encourage fresh growth.

Take care never to confuse plain-leaf parsley with the wild Fool's Parsley, which is highly poisonous. Children should only pick wild herbs when accompanied by an adult.

Culinary

Few dishes are not improved by the addition of parsley. 4 tomatoes stuffed with 3 tablespoons of chopped parsley, a clove of crushed garlic, 2 tablespoons of breadcrumbs and 2 of oil, will effectively accompany most fish or meat dishes. Parsley also brings out the flavour of other herbs and will garnish virtually anything, especially rather bland dishes. Parsley sauce is excellent with fresh vegetables, cauliflower, and Brussels sprouts, as well as fish.

Young parsley plants. 'Where parsley thrives, the woman is boss' or so the old saying goes

Medicinal

Parsley contains vitamins A, B, C, proteins, iron and other important minerals. With the exception of the seeds, all parts of the plant (including the young roots which may be eaten raw) are edible and nutritious. The herb can be taken as a general tonic and is sometimes used for anaemia. An antiseptic dressing, made by crushing the leaves, can be applied to insect bites, scratches and bruises. The lingering taste of garlic will be dispelled by chewing the fresh leaves of parsley. A tea can be made which will soothe digestive troubles and is said to ease some arthritic disorders. To make a cleansing rinse for the skin, steep a handful of chopped parsley overnight in a basin of hot water. Parsley tablets can be bought from most herbalists and are recommended by many as a urinary tonic.

Historical

The Romans wore parsley garlands at their feasts to prevent drunkenness. Because parsley is rather slow to germinate, it was believed that the seed went to the devil and back seven times before it appeared above the ground. 'Where parsley thrives, the woman is boss' — or so the saying goes.

Sweet Marjoram

Sweet (or knotted) marjoram is a low-growing annual which grows to about 9in. (22.5cm). It has small green leaves and thin woody stems. The flowers are rather odd; like little knots, tiny petals peep from green balls and look as if they are trying desperately to bloom, but they never seem quite to make it.

There are several varieties of marjoram. The most common are the sweet marjoram, pot marjoram, and wild marjoram, usually called oregano. Sweet and pot marjoram are natives of the Mediterranean area where they are perennials; in more temperate climates however, they are treated as annuals. Oregano, a much hardier plant, grows in southern England and Wales. It is also found in other countries, but its flavour varies according to the climate and habitat.

Cultivation

Read the notes on cultivation and general care, pages 9–10. Marjoram seeds, which are extremely fine, should germinate within a week to ten days. Ensure that the small plants never become too dry, or the roots will die quite quickly. Put the plants on a west or east facing windowsill; sun all day will cause the leaves to droop. Marjoram is not a hardy plant but it will survive if a little care is taken. The leaves can be gathered throughout the season.

Culinary

Sweet marjoram is milder than oregano and has a sweet, slightly peppery flavour. Dry marjoram, which is often sold in groceries, bears little resemblance in flavour to the fresh leaves. Because it is mild, this herb should be used generously in liver and other strong meat dishes — but it will be more appreciated when used with chicken and the milder meats; also with eggs and summer vegetables; and try a casserole of cubed pork with cider and garlic and a covering of chopped leaves. Marjoram blends well with thyme for stuffings and sauces and is delicious with cucumber salad; oregano blends with basil and is generally included in Italian tomato dishes as well as spaghetti bolognese and pizza.

Medicinal

Marjoram contains a volatile oil which is said to act as a mild tonic. A tea made from the fresh leaves is believed to relieve nervous headaches and encourage perspiration in feverish colds and influenza. The dried leaves are sometimes powdered and taken as snuff to clear nasal congestion. An old sixteenth-century herbal contains a medicinal recipe for Oregano sugar — the flowers and buds are chopped and added to a jar of sugar, which is left in the sun for two days. Small amounts eaten for the next two days were said to cure diseases of the eyes and kidneys. Sweet marjoram has a reputation for increasing the white blood corpuscles and generally improving circulation of the blood. An infusion can be used as a gentle face rinse.

Historical

In a Greek myth, Armarkos dropped a jar of perfume and was changed into marjoram by the gods. Venus pitied him and when she touched the plant it produced the delicate flavour and scent we know today. For centuries the herb has been used as a preserver of foods. It was believed that bunches, hung in the dairy, would prevent milk turning sour in thundery weather. Marjoram means 'joy of the mountains'.

Scented Geraniums

The two varieties of geranium illustrated opposite are the rose and the lemon. The rose has bright green, soft, slightly hairy leaves with deeply cut edges. Small pink flowers bloom in midsummer. The leaves of the lemon are similar in shape but smaller, the centres are lime-green and outer edges cream. All varieties (there are hundreds) are perennials.

Cultivation

I have yet to find a seed merchant who sells scented geranium seeds. Plants can be bought at most nurseries and particularly garden centres which specialize in the uncommon varieties. It may be advisable to buy just one plant and take a few cuttings to increase your stock. To take a cutting, detach a stem which has several pairs of leaves, cut straight across with a razor or sharp knife, just below a leaf joint. Remove leaves and buds from the lower third of the stem so that three or four pairs still remain. Use a plant pot or disposable coffee cup (depending on the size of the cutting) and fill the bottom with small pebbles for drainage. Add moist potting compost and make a hole for the cutting. Gently press down the compost round the plant and put the pot into a polythene bag. When new leaves appear, remove the bag. Re-pot when the plant becomes pot-bound (see notes on general care, page 10). Although the little flowers of scented geraniums are considered insignificant, the plants are frequently grown for the blind who particularly appreciate the perfume which is released when the leaves are gently brushed or disturbed.

Culinary

Both these geraniums have a delicate aromatic flavour with a slight tinge of spice. The washed leaves can be

chopped and added to fresh fruit salad, ice cream, plain yoghurt and cream or cottage cheese. The flavour of crab-apple jelly is greatly enhanced by placing a leaf (of either variety) at the bottom of the jar, pouring in the liquid jelly and putting another leaf on top. Seal in the usual way. The chopped (fresh or dried) leaves will give a delightful and unusual flavour when added to plain Victoria sponge mix or sponge pudding. The fresh leaves can be crushed and added to herbal teas, particularly peppermint.

Historical

The rose geranium is a native of South Africa and came to Europe in the seventeenth century. Both varieties have since been used as one of the many ingredients for potpourris. By the 1850s rose geraniums were being cultivated by the French for their expanding perfume industry.

Scented geraniums release their fragrance when touched

Sage

Sage is a hardy shrub-like perennial. Its cultivation is a peasant industry in some parts of northern Europe where it is reputed to have the highest quality. It grows wild in dry parts of the USA, along the northern shores of the Mediterranean and it is a popular pot herb in Britain, growing to approximately 24in. (60cm). Its large oval grey-green leaves release a pungent aroma when rubbed between the thumb and finger. The small flowers are usually lilac but sometimes pale blue, and bloom from May to July during the second season.

Cultivation

Read the notes on cultivation and general care, pages 9 and 10. It is said that sage is slow to grow and leaves cannot be harvested until at least a year after sowing — I must admit I have not had these problems with mine, and have gathered an abundant crop of leaves after only five months. The sage plant is hardy and may be kept outside, even during the cold winter months. At this time the plant will appear to be completely dead, but do not worry; the woody stems should be well pruned in the early spring and this will encourage new and bushy growth. The leaves are in prime condition for culinary use just before the flower spikes appear. Although sage is a perennial it should be replaced after four or five years. You can either start again from seed, or take some cuttings — see the notes on cultivation of scented geraniums on page 12.

Culinary

Sage fritters make a delicious and unusual starter. Dip the leaves in seasoned batter and fry until golden. Sage with onions, of course, makes an excellent stuffing for poultry. It is frequently added to rich or fatty dishes — roast duck, pork and eel. Sage is also used in liver, goose or duck patés, meat loaves and sausages — but do not use too much, or the strong sage flavour will overpower everything else. It can be added to fish soups and goes well in dishes whose main ingredient is cheddar cheese. Sage jelly is an interesting dessert, sometimes eaten with fresh fruit salad and home-made ice creams. A few freshly chopped leaves can also be added to any green salad. The deep-throated sage flowers are attractive to bees and produce the excellently flavoured sage honey.

Medicinal

For centuries sage has been considered one of the most important medicinal herbs. Its botanical name *Salvia* is derived from the Latin word 'salvatio'. It aids digestion (hence its use with rich and fatty dishes) and is frequently made into a medicinal tea to relieve symptoms of colds, headaches and nervous tension. The infusion can also be used as an antiseptic mouthwash for sore throats, ulcers and bleeding gums. The dried leaves can be ground into a powder and rubbed on the teeth — this is said to clean, strengthen and whiten them. Sprigs of sage, left among clothes, are believed to discourage insects and rodents. The reputation of sage is summed up in the old Arab saying — 'Why should a man die who grows sage in his garden'.

Historical

The Greeks and Romans used to rub snake bites and sores with sage leaves and even today some people use a sage infusion to treat skin ailments. The Chinese were very fond of sage tea and for many years preferred it to ordinary tea. In late Victorian times sage was recommended as a cure for dandruff.

Nasturtium

The nasturtium is a hardy annual and a well-known garden plant. There are two varieties — the dwarf which becomes quite bushy and is used for borders and window boxes; and the climber which sends off trailers and is used to cover walls or banks. Nasturtium is also grown among vegetables because many plant pests dislike the essence secreted from its roots. The flowers bloom from June to October and are brilliant red, yellow and orange.

Cultivation

Read the notes on cultivation and general care, pages 9–10. Nasturtiums are one of the easiest plants to grow. The seeds should germinate within a week of sowing. They are about the size of a dried pea, so allow only two to each coffee cup. Four or five seedlings may be transplanted into a large plant pot. The flowering season can be prolonged by removing faded blooms. It is possible to collect the seeds produced by your existing plant and keep them until the next spring, but without controlled pollination the new plants may be different and possibly inferior to the original. You could experiment using some seeds bought from a merchant and seeds produced from your plant (remember to label the pots) and compare the results. The plants will flower in abundance from midsummer until the first frosts.

Culinary

All parts of this plant — leaves, petals and seeds — have culinary uses. The leaves have a strong but not unpleasant peppery flavour. Baked in alternate layers with mushrooms and covered with a garlic dressing they make a tasty supper dish. They can also make nutritious sandwiches between slices of whole-wheat bread and butter. The fresh (not dried) flower petals

are an attractive addition to green salads — a custom originally brought from the Orient. The flower buds and petals can also be used for flavouring vinegars. The unripened fruits can be pickled like capers — but it is advisable not to eat these in large quantities.

Medicinal

The high vitamin C content of nasturtium leaves (at its peak just before flowering in July) makes the plant a valuable addition to any collection of herbs. The leaves and flowers, claimed to have blood-purifying qualities, are also taken for nervous depression, for constipation and to keep the eyes and skin clear. A hot poultice made from the crushed seeds is said to soothe boils and abscesses.

Historical

Nasturtiums were originally brought to Europe from Peru by Spanish explorers in the mid-sixteenth century. In his herbal John Gerard writes that he first received nasturtium seeds from France in 1597. Although they are Peruvian in origin, the idea of using the petals in herbal teas came from the East.

The nasturtium, a colourful and popular creeping plant whose leaves are rich in vitamin C.

Thyme

Thyme is a hardy perennial. There are many varieties, all of which have been developed from wild thyme or 'mother of thyme'. Garden thyme is the most popular because it gives superior flavour and aroma. Wild thyme flourishes in the warm, dry climate of southern Europe; the same species growing in the cooler north is less aromatic. The tiny leaves of garden thyme are grey-green and grow in pairs. The stems change from green to purple and then become wood. The main stems appear to creep along horizontally while new growth stretches upwards. Small white or mauve flowers bloom in England from May to July. The entire plant is heavily scented. It grows to a height of 8in. (20cm) and frequently the width more than doubles the height. Lemon thyme is a very popular culinary herb. Its leaves, like wild thyme, are broader than the garden variety.

Cultivation

Read the notes on cultivation and general care, pages 9–10. Thyme seeds should germinate within a week of sowing. The established plant will drink rather more water than most other herbs — but be careful not to over-water. Thyme is a sun lover and should be positioned on a south facing windowsill. Propagate by seed, cuttings or root division. Your plants should really be replaced or divided every three or four years because the aroma will gradually decrease as the plant gets older. Cut the plant back frequently to encourage bushy growth.

Culinary

Thyme is a strong-flavoured aromatic herb and should be used sparingly. Thin slices of ox liver are very tasty when coated with seasoned flour and a level tablespoon of fresh thyme leaves; served with buttered mashed potatoes and green beans. Thyme can be used in patés and sausages and makes a pleasant change when added to boiled long-grain rice. It goes well with parsley to make a white sauce for haddock and cod. Thyme is an ideal herb for dishes which are cooked slowly — stews, casseroles and hot pots — because the strong flavour is still retained throughout long simmering. Lemon thyme is rather milder than garden thyme and blends well with more delicately flavoured foods. It is also sometimes used in sweet dishes.

Medicinal

The oil from thyme has antiseptic qualities and was once an ingredient of disinfectants. A tablespoon of fresh leaves makes a pint of tea which, some say, can relieve asthmatic conditions, catarrhal bronchitis and sinus trouble. Honey, added to the tea, makes a very good cough mixture and will soothe sore throats. The infusion can also be used as a mouth wash — thyme is an ingredient of several toothpastes. The extracted oils (the most important being *thymol*), as well as having antiseptic properties, make a healthy and invigorating bath oil.

Historical

Along with certain spices and gums, thyme was burned as incense by the Greeks when worshipping in their temples. It was also used to anoint the body, being considered a symbol of courage. The association of thyme and courage also applied during the Crusades — ladies would include a sprig on the badges of bravery which they embroidered for their knights. During the Middle Ages thyme was added to other herbs and made into small posies which were carried by judges and other dignitaries to protect them from the diseases as well as the odours of the poor.

Lemon Balm

Lemon balm (Melissa balm) is a hardy perennial. It is a native of the Mediterranean but often found in southern England or Ireland. It is known as sweet balm or bee herb . The leaves are shaped like a heart, serrated and well veined (not unlike the leaves of the stinging nettle). Its small cream flowers bloom from July to September.

Cultivation

Read the notes on cultivation and general care, pages 9–10. I have often given lemon balm seeds up for lost, used the compost for other seeds and then discovered little balms springing up among thyme and basil. Be patient. See that the compost in the cups has not become dry. If it has, stand the cups in a dish of water until the compost feels moist. Lemon balm likes a sunny sheltered position, so it will be happiest on a windowsill facing west or east. It is a perennial but, as with most herbs, it is wise to propagate by seed or cuttings (see notes on cultivation of scented geraniums, page 12) before the plant becomes 'tired'. Balm can grow up to 3 feet but this is unlikely to be reached in a potted plant. It is best to keep it well cropped, compact and bushy.

Culinary

As the name suggests, balm has a lovely delicate lemon flavour. It can be used generously without any risk of overpowering most dishes. Add a handful of washed and finely chopped leaves to white sauce for chicken, ham, fish and lamb. It can be used in salads or added to cottage cheese and plain yoghurt. It gives a slight

Lemon balm — the most popular of all bee herbs.

lemony tang to desserts — crab apple jelly, apple pies and tarts, custards and fresh fruit salads. The finely chopped leaves can also be sprinkled liberally over cheese omelette and are delicious with orange mousse and grated plain chocolate. Try adding one or two bruised leaves to an iced fresh fruit drink. When baking a milk pudding cover the surface with fresh leaves after stirring in the first skin.

Medicinal

A tea made from balm leaves (fresh or dried) is said to promote relaxation, ease restless sleep and to be a mild remedy for upset stomachs and biliousness. A strong infusion added to one's bath water is extremely relaxing. Essence of lemon balm is used in toilet waters, perfumes and also furniture polish.

Historical

The Romans brought lemon balm to Britain from areas of the Mediterranean, but originally it came from the Middle East. The botanical name *Melissa* is derived from the Greek word for honey bee. The Greeks planted balm around their bee hives believing that it would encourage the bees to stay — today balm is planted in orchards as an attraction for the bees, in the hope that they will pollinate the fruit trees.

17

Mint

All varieties of mint are hardy perennials. The ones I have grown are spearmint, apple (or bowles) mint, and eau de Cologne. Spearmint grows to 18in. (45cm), has an upright stem and long, narrow, dark green leaves which are finely serrated. Apple mint can grow from 2ft.–4ft. (60cm–120cm) in height and has oval, slightly woolly leaves. Eau de Cologne has wandering stems and round, smooth green leaves with a tinge of purple. All these mints have mauvish spiked flowers which bloom from July to September. Apple mint is considered to have a superior flavour to that of spearmint. Peppermint, which has the greatest content of *menthol*, is believed to be a hybrid of spearmint and water mint. All species have certain common characteristics — they have four-sided stems, their leaves grow in pairs and they all have strong, fragrant oil.

Cultivation

It is difficult to grow mint from seed. Small plants can be bought from nurseries, or friends may offer to give you some pieces of root runner — these should be roughly 4in.–6in. (10cm–15cm) long and will need to go into a fairly large pot. (The three varieties which I grow are planted in half of an old beer barrel which stands outside my kitchen door.) Plant the runners 2in. (5cm) deep in potting compost. Spring or autumn is the best planting time, but mint is hardy and will root at almost any time. Put the pot on a windowsill facing south, east or west. Do not allow the plants to grow too tall, and nip out the flowers as they appear.

Culinary

Mint is a world-wide culinary herb — in Europe it is traditionally eaten with lamb, duck and spring vegetables, particularly new potatoes; in India it is included in highly spiced dishes and chutneys; in the Middle East it is combined with pulses and yoghurt. Spearmint is used mainly in mint sauce or jelly which accompanies roast lamb. An excellent sauce can be made by combining spearmint and apple mint with wine vinegar or cider. Apple mint is delicious when shredded over salads or mixed into cottage cheese or plain yoghurt. Eau de Cologne is rather special — add it to sweet omelettes and soufflés, fresh fruit salad, or as a garnish for cool summer drinks. An infusion of leaves can be added to jellies made with fresh orange juice. The leaves of all varieties will add savour when rubbed into roast meat joints and poultry. All in all, mint is an essential plant for anyone interested in culinary herbs.

Medicinal

Fresh mint leaves are said to bring some relief when rubbed gently onto an aching head or rheumatic joints. Peppermint leaves, containing *menthol* which is an antiseptic and anaesthetic, can be chewed to relieve toothache. An infusion of peppermint leaves (a well known French tisane) is very good for indigestion and for settling the stomach after an attack of vomiting. An infusion of spearmint can be used as a rinsing lotion to improve the complexion.

Historical

According to Greek mythology, Pluto, God of the Underworld, loved a nymph, Menthe. Pluto's wife became jealous and turned her into the plant which bears her name. The Arabs have taken mint tea for centuries, believing that it would stimulate their virility. In his herbal John Gerard wrote — 'Mint is wholesome for the stomach. It is good for watering eyes. It is poured into the ears with honied water.' Pennyroyal, another variety of mint, was used as an ointment which warded off fleas and other insects.

Summer Savory

There are two varieties of savory — summer and winter. Of the two, summer savory is the better for culinary use. It is a tender annual rarely found in Britain, but which grows wild in the warmer parts of Europe. It can reach a height of 24in. (60cm). The small narrow leaves, covered with oil glands, grow sparsely along the rigid stems. Tiny mauve or white flowers are produced in the axils of the leaves and bloom from July to September. The flowers are attractive to bees.

Winter savory is a perennial, a shrubby plant which grows to about 12in. (30cm). The leaves are similar to those of summer savory, but more pointed, with a shiny upper surface. Its flowers are also attractive to bees. The plant can usually survive the winter, but it will have a better chance inside the house.

Cultivation

Read the notes on cultivation and general care, pages 9–10. The seeds should germinate within a week or ten days of sowing (but can sometimes take a little longer). If they are sown in May or June the plant will be ready to use with home-grown beans. Summer savory enjoys a sunny position, so place the pot on a windowsill facing south, east or west. Take care not to squash the pot between other plants because its growth will be easily retarded. It is better not to allow the plant to grow to its full height — keep it well cropped and compact. The leaves can be picked throughout the summer. Winter savory can be

Summer savory — in Europe the 'bean herb'.

propagated by seed, cuttings or root division. The plants often become straggly and need severe pruning.

Culinary

The leaves of summer savory have a peppery, spicy taste. During the Middle Ages the plant was used for flavouring trout, but it is now thought of as the traditional bean herb. Haricot, runner, French and broad beans are all improved by the addition of savory which brings out the flavour (particularly if the beans are frozen) and helps digestion. The herb is also used, because of its warming spicy flavour, in sausages, meat pies, stuffings and thick vegetable soups. Add freshly chopped leaves to cucumber salad and cheese dishes; it makes a very good herb vinegar.

Medicinal

Summer savory contains an oil which aids digestion. An infusion made from the fresh or dried leaves is said to dispel wind and regularize the bowels. The fresh leaves, when rubbed on a wasp sting, bring immediate relief.

Historical

The Romans, who introduced the savories to Britain, used them before the hot oriental spices were imported. The plants then became popular culinary herbs for the Saxons. A sauce used to be made with savory and vinegar very similar to our mint sauce.

Home-baked breads

Introduction

It is amazing how the smell of baking bread can stir the imagination. On a late winter's afternoon, when we open the door of a warm, brightly lit kitchen where bread is being baked, the aroma and atmosphere are heavenly — feelings of nostalgia and delight suddenly overwhelm us (even if we have never experienced it before we like to think of childhood days, comforting, homely, secure). On such winter's days, during my 12-hour bread-making sessions, I often take my four young children out for a brisk walk in the park, just in order to experience that magical home-coming.

At the start of this century bread-making was one of a housewife's main occupations, but as small bakeries became larger and housewives' interests extended beyond the kitchen, making bread became a less important part of the daily routine. Now, however, people are beginning to tire of the standard packaged, pre-sliced and vitamin-added loaf and not only because prices are higher; they are going back to home-made foods, because convenience foods are often unimaginatively prepared, have little, or no, authentic flavour and contain unnecessary additives.

Making bread is not difficult. My family's daily bread (*Quick wholewheat*, page 22) takes only seven minutes to prepare. Then, after a rising on top of the oven for half an hour or so, I pop it in the oven; forty minutes later we have a tray of nourishing, crusty, warm loaves, and at only half the cost of shop bread.

Youngsters love playing with bread dough, especially the plain white dough which is springy, smooth and soft. My children line up on the kitchen bench to compare the dough sausages, pancakes and flowers they have made. They eat their misshapen attempts with great relish.

This chapter contains a variety of recipes. Some are more ambitious than others but all are wholesome. Once you have baked and eaten your own bread, you will never again be satisfied with a shop bought loaf.

Notes and hints

Yeast. All the recipes in this chapter ask for fresh yeast; if you cannot get it, use dry yeast and halve the quantity. For example: in place of 1oz (30 grams) fresh yeast, use ½oz (15g) dry yeast. Other ingredients remain the same.

Warm water. For any quantity of warm water use two parts cold to one part boiling. Never use the water from a hot-water tap.

Flour. Do not be afraid to use less expensive brands of flour. I have found no noticeable difference.

Cholesterol. If you are worried about the cholesterol content of butter, use a soft margarine containing a reduced amount of animal fat, or none at all (but check the current composition of each brand).

Spice. The flavour of a spiced bread is more piquant if you buy the whole spices and grind them as you need them. A coffee grinder is ideal for this purpose.

The various flours, dried fruits and herbs can be bought from most health-food stores.

Testing. If you are not sure when your bread is baked, remove it from the tin and tap the bottom of the loaf. If it sounds hollow it is baked; if not, pop it back in the oven for 5–10 minutes longer.

Oil. The easiest way to oil a polythene bag is to lay it flat, oil the facing side then turn it inside out.

'Prove'. The word refers simply to a second rising. *Quick wholewheat* (page 22) does not require this.

If you begin to make bread regularly you will soon discover short-cuts and other methods to suit you personally. I find it easier to spend a whole day and evening baking 60 loaves, then I freeze them and make another batch a month later. Confidence has a great deal to with good bread-making, so be confident, and if your first attempt is a bit of a flop, have a laugh and start again — you will soon master it.

Basic white bread — recipe on page 22

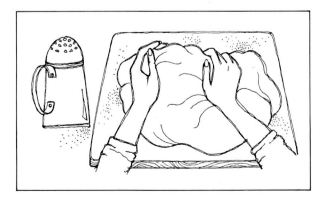

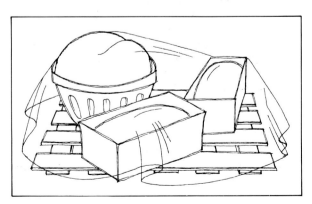

Basic equipment for bread-making

You will need: a large mixing basin (I use a plastic washing-up bowl which is easier to handle than the normal pastry basin and prevents any spillage of flour when doing the initial mixing); large metal spoon; wooden spoon; measuring spoons; measuring jug; plastic spatula; 1lb and 2lb loaf tins; baking sheets; polythene bags; pastry brush; wire cooling tray.

Basic white bread

1oz (30g) fresh yeast
1½pt (850ml) warm water
1 tblsp sugar
3lb (1kg 340g) plain flour
1 tblsp salt
2oz (55g) butter
beaten egg for glaze

Crumble the yeast in a jug. Add a sprinkling of the sugar and cream to a paste with a little of the water. When the yeast is frothy (5 minutes) add the remaining water. Mix the flour, salt and sugar in a basin and rub in the butter. Make a well in the centre and pour in the yeast liquid. Mix thoroughly with a large spoon. Scraping the sides of the basin clean with a spatula, turn the dough on to a lightly floured surface. Knead for 7 minutes. The dough should be smooth and elastic. Return it to the basin, cover with a lightly oiled polythene bag and set in a warm draught-free place for 1½ hours. The dough should have doubled in bulk.

Oil a 1lb and 2lb loaf tin and two baking sheets.

Turn the dough onto a lightly floured surface and knead for 7 minutes. Weigh 14oz (390g) of dough and knead, tucking the dough underneath itself so that the surface is smooth. Place it in the 1lb tin.

Weigh 1lb (450g) of dough. Knead and tuck into a round. Place on one of the baking sheets.

Weigh three 8oz (225g) pieces of dough. Knead and form into balls, tucking as before. Place side by side in a 2lb loaf tin.

Divide the remaining dough into eight. Knead, tuck into rounds and place on the second baking sheet.

Cover all the dough with the polythene bag and prove in a warm, draught-free place for 45 minutes.

Pre-heat the oven to 425° (220°C), gas mark 7. Brush the bread with beaten egg. Place the bread buns on the second shelf from the top, with the cob underneath. The bread buns should take 20–25 minutes. When they are baked put the cob in their place and the tinned loaves underneath. The cob and small loaf will take about 45 minutes, the large loaf about 5–10 minutes longer. Let the bread cool on a wire tray.

Quick wholewheat

1oz (30g) fresh yeast
1½pt (850ml) warm water
1 tblsp brown sugar
3lb (1kg 340g) wholewheat flour
1 tblsp salt
5 tblsp vegetable oil
small beaten egg and
  wheatgerm for glaze (optional)

Cream together the yeast, sugar and a little of the warm water in a large jug. When the yeast is frothy (5–10 minutes) add the remaining water. Mix the flour and salt in a warm basin. Make a well in the centre and pour in the yeast liquid. When the ingredients are partially mixed add the oil and bind together with a large spoon. Scrape the sides of the basin clean with a spatula, turn the dough out onto a lightly floured surface and knead for 7 minutes. Lightly oil two 1lb and two 2lb loaf tins. Divide the dough into four, (two portions being rather smaller than the other two). Place the smaller portions in the 1lb tins and the larger portions in the 2lb tins. Cover with a lightly oiled polythene bag and set in a warm, draught-free place for 2 hours. Bake the loaves at 425°F (220°C), gas mark 7, for 35–40 minutes.

For an unusual change you can bake the loaves in flower-pots. Use scrupulously clean clay pots, greased with cold butter. Cut a circle of thick greaseproof paper slightly larger than the pot base. Snip ¼in. (6mm) cuts round the edge of the circle and position it in the bottom of the pot. Cut strips a little longer than the height of the pot and tapering at one end. Stick these, narrow end down, inside the pot, overlapping them slightly. Snip ¼in. (6mm) cuts into the paper which stands above the pot. Take a portion of the dough about half the size of the pot, and form it into a smooth crack-free ball. Place this in the pot and cover with a lightly oiled polythene bag. Leave to rise in a warm place for 2 hours, or until the dough has risen slightly above the pots. Bake the loaves at 450°F (230°C), gas mark 8, for 10 minutes. Remove, brush with beaten egg and sprinkle with the wheatgerm. Return to the oven at 400°F (200°C), gas mark 6, and bake for a further 30 minutes.

Herb and onion bread

¾oz (22g) fresh yeast
1 teasp sugar
8fl.oz (230ml) warm water
4fl.oz (110ml) milk
2oz (60g) butter
1¼lb (560g) wholewheat flour
1½ teasp salt
2 medium onions
1½ teasp each of dried basil, sage and oregano

Crumble the yeast into a cup and sprinkle with the sugar. Add 2 tablespoons of the warm water and mix until smooth. Set in a warm place for 10 minutes, or until the mixture becomes frothy.

Pour the milk into a small pan and heat gently. Remove from heat just before the milk begins to boil. Chop the butter and drop it into the milk. Add the remaining water. Leave for 10 minutes or until the butter has melted and the milk is lukewarm.

Peel the onions and finely mince or grate them. Put the flour and salt into a large basin. Add the herbs and

Herb and onion bread, perfect for cold meat sandwiches

onions. Mix thoroughly. Make a well in the centre and pour in the yeast and milk. With a wooden spoon, gradually work the mixture to a soft dough. Scrape the basin clean with a plastic spatula, and turn the dough on to a lightly floured working surface and knead for 10 minutes. Return the dough to the basin, cover with a damp tea towel and leave in a warm, draught-free place for 2 hours or until the dough has doubled its original size.

Oil two 1lb loaf tins. Turn the dough on to a lightly floured surface and knead for 7 minutes. Divide into two equal portions and shape into loaves. Place in the tins, cover with a damp tea towel and leave in a warm place for 45 minutes or until the dough has almost doubled in bulk.

Pre-heat the oven to 350°F (180°C), gas mark 4. Put the loaves in the centre of the oven and bake for 45 minutes. Increase the heat to 425°F (220°C), gas mark 7, and bake for a further 30 minutes. Remove from the tins and cool on a wire tray.

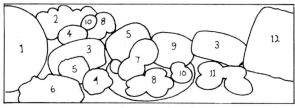

Buckwheat hotcakes

½oz (15g) fresh yeast
½ teasp sugar
4 tblsp warm water
½pt (280ml) milk
7 tblsp plain flour
6oz (170g) buckwheat flour
½ teasp salt
3 eggs
1 teasp caster sugar
1oz (30g) butter

Buckwheat flour can be bought from most health-food stores. It is very nutritious, containing thiamine, iron and a high proportion of protein.

Cream the yeast, sugar and water to a paste in a basin. Leave until frothy (5 minutes), then add half of the milk and the plain flour. Beat the mixture to a smooth batter. Cover with a dry cloth and leave in a warm, draught-free place for 2 hours.

Beat the eggs, sugar and remaining milk in a large basin. Add the yeast mixture, then slowly work in the buckwheat flour and salt. Beat to a smooth batter. Melt the butter in a pan and add to the batter. Beat.

Have ready a hot griddle, hot plate or sturdy baking sheet, lightly oiled. Spoon 5 or 6 separate tablespoons of the batter on to the griddle and leave until small bubbles appear. Turn the cakes over with a fish slice and brown for a few minutes. Put the cakes on a wire tray to cool. Lightly oil the griddle for each batch of cakes. (Makes about 50 hotcakes.)

Orange and aniseed bread

3 large oranges
8fl.oz (230ml) milk
1oz (30g) fresh yeast
2lb (900g) strong plain flour
1 tblsp sugar
3 teasp aniseed
6oz (170g) butter
3 eggs
2 teasp salt
5 tblsp caster sugar
2 tblsp milk

Grate the orange onto a plate using a fine grater and taking only the bright orange zest. Leave the plate on one side. Cut the oranges in half and squeeze the juice into a measuring jug. Add enough warm water to make 6fl.oz (170ml) of liquid.

Put the milk in a small pan and heat gently until warm. Crumble the yeast into a large basin. Stir in the sugar and 8oz (220g) of the flour. Make a well in the centre and, using a wooden spoon, stir in the warm milk. When the ingredients are partially mixed add the orange juice. Mix thoroughly, then cover with a damp cloth. Set in a warm, draught-free place for 45 minutes. Grind the aniseed coarsely.

Put the butter in a small pan and heat gently until melted. Break the eggs into a cup and beat lightly with a fork. Using a wooden spoon, add the butter and eggs to the yeast mixture, then gradually work in the salt, caster sugar, ground aniseed, grated orange peel and the remaining flour. Mix well until a soft dough is formed. Turn onto a lightly floured working surface and knead for 7 minutes. Form into a smooth ball and return to the basin. Cover with a damp cloth and set in a warm, draught-free place for an hour, or until the dough has almost doubled its original size.

Oil two baking sheets. Turn the dough out of the basin, knead for 5 minutes, then cut into four equal portions. Form the portions into fat rolls, about 6in. (15cm) long. Place on the baking sheets and cut 3 lines on the top of each roll with a very sharp knife. Cover with a damp tea towel and leave in a warm place until almost doubled in size.

Pre-heat the oven to 425°F (220°C), gas mark 7. Brush the rolls with milk and bake in the centre of the oven for 40 minutes. Cool on a wire tray.

Cheese and celery plait

¾oz (20g) fresh yeast
10fl.oz (285ml) warm water
1 teasp sugar
1lb (450g) plain flour
1 teasp each of salt, dry mustard
   and paprika pepper
1 tblsp celery seeds
5oz (140g) grated cheddar cheese
1 beaten egg for glaze

Cream the yeast and sugar in a jug with a little of the water. When the yeast is frothy add the remaining water. Mix the flour, salt, mustard and paprika pepper in a basin. Add the celery seeds and 4oz (110g) of the grated cheese. Make a well in the centre and pour in the yeast liquid. Mix thoroughly. Scrape the sides of the basin clean with a spatula and turn the dough onto a lightly floured surface. Knead for 7 minutes. The dough should be elastic and smooth. Return it to the basin and cover with a lightly oiled polythene bag. Set in a warm, draught-free place for 1½ hours.

Turn the dough onto a lightly floured surface and knead for 5 minutes. Cut the dough in half. Divide the first half into 3 equal portions. Roll each portion into a sausage then gently pull them from hand to hand so that they are the same width all the way down. They

Cheese and celery plaits — ideal picnic bread

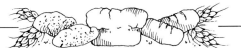

should be about 9in. (23cm) long. Lay them vertically 1in. (25mm) apart, nip firmly together at the top and work a plait, nipping again at the end. Transfer the plait onto an oiled baking sheet with the spatula. Repeat this process with the remaining dough. Cover with the polythene bag and prove in a warm, draught-free place for 45 minutes.

Pre-heat the oven to 425°F (220°C), gas mark 7. with beaten egg and sprinkle on the remaining grated cheese. Reduce the heat to 400°F (200°C), gas mark 6 and bake for a further 30 minutes.

Almost an Italian meal, tomato and oregano loaves

Tomato and oregano loaves

¾oz (20g) fresh yeast
2fl.oz (55ml) warm water
1 teasp sugar
8fl.oz (225ml) tomato juice
1lb (450g) plain flour
2 teasp salt
1oz (30g) butter
2 teasp dried oregano
beaten egg and salt for glaze

Crumble the yeast into a small jug. Add the sugar and cream to a paste with the warm water. Pour the tomato juice into a pan and heat gently until

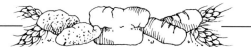

lukewarm. Mix the flour, salt and dried oregano in a basin and rub in the butter. Make a well in the centre then pour in the yeast liquid and tomato juice. Combine all the ingredients thoroughly. Scrape the sides of the basin clean with a plastic or rubber spatula and turn the dough out onto a lightly floured surface. Knead for ten minutes. Return the dough to the basin in the form of a smooth ball and cover with a lightly oiled polythene bag or sheet. Set on top of a warm oven (or in a warm airing cupboard) for 1–1½ hours. The dough should have doubled in bulk.

Have prepared two oiled baking sheets. Scrape the sides of the bowl clean with the spatula and turn the dough out onto a lightly floured surface. Knead for 5 minutes. Divide into two portions and, tucking the dough underneath itself so that the top surface is smooth, shape into two fat sausages, each a little shorter than the baking sheets. Place on the baking sheets and with a sharp knife cut four diagonal slits ⅜in. (1cm) deep on each loaf. Cover with the polythene and prove in a warm place for 45 minutes.

Pre-heat the oven to 375°F (190°C), gas mark 5. Place the loaves in the centre of the oven and bake for 30 minutes. Meanwhile, beat the egg in a small cup or bowl and mix in a sprinkling of salt and a little dried oregano (optional). Remove the loaves from the oven and brush liberally with the glaze. Return and bake for a further 30 minutes.

Crispy bread sticks

½oz (15g) fresh yeast
5fl.oz (140ml) warm water
8oz (225g) plain flour
1 teasp salt
beaten egg and
    sesame seeds for glaze

Crumble the yeast into a small basin and cream to a paste with a little of the warm water. Stir in the remaining water. Mix the flour and salt in a basin. Make a well in the centre and pour in the liquid yeast. Combine the ingredients thoroughly. Scrape the sides of the basin clean with a spatula, and turn the dough out onto a lightly floured surface. Knead for 10 minutes, dipping occasionally into the flour bag if the dough seems over-sticky. The dough should be smooth and elastic. Return it to the basin and cover with a lightly oiled polythene bag. Set on top of a warm oven for 1 hour. The dough should have doubled in bulk.

Turn the dough out onto a lightly floured surface and knead for 5 minutes. Shape the dough into an oblong and, using a lightly floured rolling pin, roll, stretch and pull until it is slightly less than ⅛in. (3mm) thick. Continue rolling, stretching and pulling until the dough is smooth and retains its shape without springing back. Leave to settle for a few minutes and prepare 3 baking sheets brushed with oil. Trim the edges of the dough to make a neat oblong (the trimmings may be used later to make more sticks), then cut into strips ⅜in. (1cm) wide. Twist these gently and place them on the baking sheets about 1in. (2½cm) apart. Press the ends down firmly to prevent them from springing out of shape. Pre-heat the oven to 450°F (220°C), gas mark 8. Prove the bread sticks on top of the oven, uncovered, for 20 minutes. Brush carefully with beaten egg and sprinkle liberally with sesame seeds. For a pale golden stick, bake for 10 minutes. For a deeper colour and crunchy texture, bake for a further 6 minutes.

Butter pikelets

1pt (570ml) milk
½oz (15g) fresh yeast
½ teasp sugar
1lb (450g) plain flour
½ teasp salt
3oz (80g) butter
1 egg

You will need 6 pikelet (or crumpet) rings and a griddle or sturdy baking sheet for this recipe. The rings and griddle can be bought from most kitchen equipment shops and some hardware stores.

Pour the milk into a pan and heat gently until just warm. Crumble the yeast into a cup and sprinkle with the sugar. Add 2 tablespoons of the warm milk and mix until smooth. Leave in a warm place for 10 minutes or until the mixture becomes frothy.

Sift the flour and salt into a large basin. Put 1oz (30g) of the butter into a small pan and heat gently until melted. Make a well in the centre of the flour and pour in the yeast, the remaining warm milk, the beaten egg and melted butter. With a wooden spoon work the

Pikelets, traditionally toasted over an open fire

ingredients to a smooth batter. Cover the basin with a dry tea towel and set in a warm, draught-free place (on top of a warm oven, in a warm airing cupboard or next to a warm radiator) for about 45 minutes, or until the batter has doubled in volume.

Melt the remaining butter in a small pan. Brush the griddle, or baking sheet, and the pikelet rings with the butter. Position the rings on the griddle and place over a moderate heat. When the rings feel hot, reduce the heat to low. Stir the batter lightly then drop 2 tablespoons of it into each ring. Cook the pikelets for 8 minutes, or until the tops are set and full of small holes and the undersides are golden brown. Transfer to a wire tray with the help of a fish slice and leave until cold. To serve the pikelets, toast both sides on an open fire or under a grill for about 6 minutes. Butter liberally and eat while still warm. Makes about 25.

Brioche

1oz (30g) fresh yeast
5fl.oz (140ml) warm water
10oz (285ml) milk
1 tbsp sugar
2 teasp salt
1½lb (670g) plain flour
8oz (225g) softened butter
5 eggs
1 egg yolk and
1 tbslp milk for glaze

*Brioche buns — a delicious part of the typical
French breakfast. Serve fresh, with hot black coffee*

Heat the milk almost to boiling point, then cool it until it is lukewarm. Cream the yeast and sugar with a little of the water in a large warm basin. When the yeast is frothy (5–10 minutes) stir in the remaining water, the milk and salt. Add one-third of the flour and the butter, and beat. Add a portion of the remaining flour and one egg. Beat thoroughly and continue adding a portion of the flour with one egg, beating after each addition. Beat the batter for 20 minutes. Grab the dough and pull it out of the basin then slap it back. Repeat for 5 minutes until the dough starts to come away from your hands. Scrape your hands and the sides of the basin with a spatula. Pat the dough into a smooth round and cover with a lightly oiled polythene bag. Set in a warm, draught-free place for 1½ hours.

The dough should have doubled in bulk.

Mix the dough with a spatula. Keeping your hands lightly floured, pull away eight 1oz (30g) pieces. Form these into balls and place them on a lightly floured baking sheet. Pull away eight ½oz (15g) pieces, form into balls and place on the same sheet. Cover with a dry tea towel. Make two balls with the remaining dough, one being about a quarter the size of the other. Place each in a basin and cover with a dry tea towel. Put the covered baking sheet and basins in the fridge. Leave for at least 6 hours but preferably overnight.

Butter 8 small and 1 large brioche tins. Put the eight 1oz (30g) balls into the small tins. Make a hole in the centre of each with a floured finger. Form the smaller balls into peardrops and put them, point down, into the holes. Repeat this process with the two larger balls. Cover with the polythene bag and prove in a warm, draught-free place for about 25 minutes. Pre-heat the oven to 475°F (240°C), gas mark 9. Place the buns in the centre of the oven and bake for 20 minutes. Remove and, avoiding the joints where the peardrops have been pushed into the main bun, brush with the beaten egg yolk and milk. Reduce the oven heat to 400°F (200°C), gas mark 6. Return the buns and bake the little brioches for 20 minutes and the large brioches for 40 minutes.

Salty pretzels and croissants

¾oz (20g) fresh yeast
7fl.oz (200ml) warm water
3fl.oz (85ml) evaporated milk
1 tblsp sugar
1lb (450g) plain flour
3 tblsp vegetable oil
2 teasp salt
beaten egg for glaze

Cream the yeast and sugar with a little of the water in a large basin. When the yeast is frothy (5 minutes) add the remaining water, evaporated milk, oil, salt and half of the flour. Beat well and add the remaining flour gradually. Scrape the sides of the basin clean, and turn the dough out onto a lightly floured surface and knead for 10 minutes. The dough should be smooth and elastic. Return it to the basin and cover it with a lightly oiled polythene bag. Set in a warm place for 1 hour or until the dough has doubled in bulk.

Turn the dough out onto a lightly floured surface. Knead for 5 minutes, then cut in half. Take the first half and make four equal balls. Put these aside and with the second half make fourteen 1oz (30g) balls. Return to the four balls, take one and, using a lightly floured rolling pin, roll it into an 8in. (20cm) circle (cut round a plate). Cut the circle into 8 wedges. Starting with the wide end, roll each wedge tightly. Place on an oiled baking sheet with points underneath. Repeat with the other three balls. Pre-heat the oven to 425°F (220°C), gas mark 7. Prove the croissants, uncovered, for 10 minutes on top of the oven. Brush with the egg and sprinkle with salt. Bake for 15 minutes.

Return to the little balls. Roll one into a 12in. (30cm) sausage. Make a circle, cross the ends over each other once, then once again. Lift the ends up and attach them to the opposite side of the circle. Place on an oiled baking sheet. Repeat with the remaining balls. Leave to prove for 10 minutes, uncovered, on top of the oven. Brush with the beaten egg, sprinkle with salt and bake for 25 minutes.

Persian nut bread

1oz (30g) fresh yeast
1 teasp sugar
1pt (570ml) milk
2lb (900g) plain flour
2 teasp salt
2 tblsp cooking oil
4oz (110g) shelled peanuts
3oz (80g) each of shelled pinenuts,
    walnuts, almonds and hazel nuts
3 tblsp sesame seeds
3 teasp poppy seeds
1 teasp each of cumin and fennel
20 black peppercorns
4 egg yolks
2 teasp cooking salt
2 tblsp grated parmesan

Put the milk in a pan and heat until warm. Crumble the yeast into a cup and sprinkle with the sugar. Add 3 tablespoons of the milk. Leave in a warm place for 5

minutes, or until the mixture becomes frothy.

Sift the flour and salt into a large basin and make a well in the centre. Work in the yeast, remaining milk and the oil. Work the mixture to a soft dough then turn onto a lightly floured surface, scraping the basin clean with a spatula. Knead the dough for 10 minutes. Place in the basin and cover with a damp cloth. Set in a warm, draught-free place for 1½ hours or until the dough has doubled in bulk.

Meanwhile, prepare the topping. Put the peanuts in a dish and cover with boiling water. Leave for a few minutes, then drain, remove the skins, and split in half. Put them in a basin with the pinenuts. Chop th₁ walnuts, almonds and hazel nuts finely. Add them to the peanuts, together with the sesame and poppy seeds. Roughly grind the cumin, fennel and peppercorns and add them to the basin. Mix well. Put the egg yolks in cup and beat lightly. Pour on to the

Persian nut bread. Unusual savoury bread from the East

nuts and mix. Put the basin to one side until the dough is ready.

Oil two large baking sheets. Turn the dough out of the basin and knead for 6 minutes. Cut in half and form into two balls. Place a ball in the centre of each sheet and flatten to 1in. (2½cm) thick. Pre-heat the oven to 450°F (240°C), gas mark 9.

Using a fork, spread the topping over the cakes to within ¾in. (2cm) of the edge. Sprinkle with the salt, then with the cheese. Bake in the centre of the oven for 15 minutes. Lower the heat to 400°F (200°C), gas mark 6, and bake on the lowest shelves for 45 minutes. To brown the underside of the cakes, remove from the baking sheets, place on the open shelves, and bake for a further 15 minutes. Remove, and cool on a wire tray.

Newcastle lardy cake

½oz (15g) fresh yeast
1 teasp sugar
½pt (280ml) warm water
1lb (450g) plain flour
1 teasp salt
1 tblsp cooking oil
2oz (60g) lard
2oz (60g) butter
4oz (110g) currants
4oz (110g) caster sugar
1 teasp mixed ground spice
1 tblsp cooking oil and
   1 tblsp caster sugar for glaze

Cream the yeast and the teaspoonful of sugar in a jug, with 3 tablespoons of the warm water. Leave until the yeast begins to froth, then add the remaining warm water. Put the flour and salt in a basin. Make a well in the centre and pour in the yeast mixture. When the ingredients are partially mixed add the cooking oil. Mix thoroughly and turn out onto a lightly floured surface, scraping the basin clean with a spatula. Knead the dough for 5 minutes — it should be smooth and elastic. Return it to the basin and cover with a damp tea towel. Set in a warm, draught-free place for 1 hour, or until the dough has doubled in bulk.

Turn the dough onto a lightly floured surface and knead for 10 minutes. Dust a rolling pin with flour and roll the dough to an oblong, 15in. (38cm) long, 7in. (18cm) wide and ½in. (1½cm) thick. Slice half of the lard and half of the butter into thin flakes and dot them over two-thirds of the dough. Mix the currants, caster sugar and spice together and sprinkle half the mixture over the flakes. Press them into the dough. Fold the dough twice to form a square, folding the plain third of the dough down first. Turn the dough round and roll into another oblong. Flake the remaining fats over two-thirds of the dough. Sprinkle the remaining currant mixture over the flakes and press gently. Fold as before. Oil an 8in. (20cm) baking tin and carefully fit the dough in, pushing it into the corners. Cover with a damp tea towel and leave in a warm draught-free place for 1½ hours.

Brush the dough with the tablespoon of oil and sprinkle with caster sugar. Score neat criss-cross lines over the surface with a sharp-pointed knife. Bake in the centre of a hot oven, 425°F (220°C), gas mark 7, for 40–45 minutes, or until the cake is a rich golden brown. Cool on a wire tray.

Peasant's black bread

¾oz (20g) fresh yeast
4fl.oz (110ml) warm water
16fl.oz (455ml) hot water
1 teasp sugar
3 teasp postum
8oz (225g) plain flour
1lb (450g) rye flour
6oz (170g) dry bread crumbs
4 tblsp molasses
2oz (55g) butter
2 teasp salt
1oz (30g) wheatgerm
1 teasp ground ginger
3 teasp ground coriander

Sprinkle the bread crumbs evenly on a clean baking sheet and bake in the centre of the oven at 400°F (200°C), gas mark 6, until they are quite parched. Pour the hot water into a basin. Add the postum and stir until it dissolves. Stir in the molasses and bread crumbs. Leave on one side until the bread crumbs are soft and the liquid is lukewarm.

Crumble the yeast into a small jug. Add the sugar and mix to a paste with a little of the warm water. When the yeast is frothy (5–10 minutes) add the remaining water. Mix the two flours, wheatgerm, salt, ground ginger and ground coriander in a warm basin. Rub in the butter. Make a well in the centre and pour in the yeast liquid and bread crumb mixture. Combine the ingredients thoroughly using a large spoon. The dough will be very sticky. Scraping the sides of the basin clean with a spatula, bring the dough into the centre and pat into a round. Cover with a lightly oiled polythene bag or sheet and set in a warm place (on top of a warm oven, in a warm airing cupboad or next to a warm radiator) for 2–3 hours. The dough should have almost doubled in bulk.

Have prepared three baking sheets brushed with oil or melted butter. Scrape the sides of the basin clean with the spatula and turn the dough out onto a lightly floured surface. Dipping your hands occasionally into the flour bag, knead for 7 minutes. Cut the dough into three portions, roughly 1½lb (670g) each. Knead and pat, and gently form into rounds. Place each on a baking sheet, cover with the polythene and prove in a warm place for 30 minutes. Pre-heat the oven to 400°F (200°C), gas mark 6. Brush the loaves with a mixture of one teaspoon of postum dissolved in two teaspoons of warm water. Sprinkle with wheatgerm and bake for 45 minutes. Cool on a wire tray.

If you intend baking this bread regularly you can make each successive loaf darker by saving the crusts and crumbling them into bread crumbs. Toast them and store in the freezer for the next batch of bread.

Fruity Chelsea buns

1lb (450g) strong plain flour
2 teasp sugar
½oz (15g) fresh yeast
8fl.oz (230ml) milk
1 teasp salt
4oz (110g) butter
2 eggs
4 tblsp soft brown sugar
4 tblsp chopped mixed peel
4 tblsp raisins or sultanas
3 tblsp currants
2 teasp ground mixed spice
3–4 tblsp clear honey

Measure the milk into a pan and heat it gently until warm. Crumble the yeast into a basin. Mix in 4oz (110g) of the flour and the white sugar. Using a wooden spoon, gradually work in the warm milk, then beat to a smooth batter. Cover the basin with a damp cloth and leave in a warm, draught-free place for about 20 minutes or until the mixture becomes frothy.

Sift the remaining flour and the salt into a basin. Rub in 2½oz (75g) of the butter. Break the eggs into a cup and beat lightly. Make a well in the centre of the flour and gradually work in the eggs and yeast mixture. Work until a soft dough is formed. Turn onto a lightly floured surface, scraping the basin clean with a spatula. Knead for 10 minutes, the dough should be soft, smooth and elastic. Return it to the basin and cover with a damp tea towel. Set in a warm, draught-free place for 1½ hours, or until the dough has almost doubled its original size.

Mix the brown sugar, chopped peel, raisins,

A traditional English favourite, fruity Chelsea buns

currants and spice in a basin. Put the remaining butter in a small pan and heat gently until melted.

Oil two baking sheets. Turn the dough onto a lightly floured surface and knead for 5 minutes. Dust a rolling pin with flour and roll the dough to an oblong 11in. × 14in. (28cm × 36cm). Brush the surface with the melted butter and sprinkle the fruit to within ½in. (1½cm) of the edges. Taking one of the longer sides,

roll the dough fairly tightly. Nip firmly but neatly to seal the roll. Using a very sharp knife, cut the roll into slices about 1in. (2½cm) thick and place on the baking sheets. Cover with a dry cloth and set in a warm, draught-free place for 35 minutes. Pre-heat the oven to 425°F (220°C), gas mark 7. Bake the buns in the centre of the oven for 35 minutes. Place on a wire tray and brush with honey while still hot.

Irish soda bread

2lb (900g) plain flour
2 teasp salt
3 teasp bicarbonate of soda
17fl.oz (480ml) buttermilk
1oz (30g) butter

This bread needs no yeast and no rising or proving. Eaten while still warm, with lashings of butter and home-made blackberry jelly, it is delicious — an ideal treat for the children when they come home from school on a cold winter's afternoon.

Pre-heat the oven to 425°F (220°C), gas mark 7. Sift the flour, salt and bicarbonate of soda into a large basin. With a wooden spoon gradually work in the buttermilk. Combine the mixture thoroughly — the dough should be smooth but firmer than normal bread dough. Turn onto a lightly floured surface and knead lightly for 3–4 minutes. Divide the dough into two equal portions. Form each portion into a firm ball then gently press with the palm of your hand to a flat round cake, about 8in. (20cm) across and 1½in. (4cm) thick. Generously butter two baking sheets and position a cake in the centre of each. Cut a deep cross, extending to the edges, on the top of each cake. Place in the centre of the oven and bake for 35 minutes or until pale golden.

Transfer the loaves to a wire tray. Leave to cool for 30 minutes and eat them while still slightly warm.

Cardamom round loaf

¾oz (20g) fresh yeast
4fl.oz (110ml) warm water
4oz (110g) sugar
1½lb (670g) plain flour
10fl.oz (285ml) milk
4oz (110g) butter
1 large egg
2 teasp salt
2 teasp ground cardamom
6oz (170g) seedless raisins
2oz (55g) chopped citron
3oz (85g) flaked almonds
beaten egg for glaze

Pour the milk in a pan and heat to almost boiling point. Remove the pan and add the butter and sugar, stirring until the butter is melted and the sugar dissolved. Cool the liquid to lukewarm by placing the pan in a bowl of cold water. Crumble the yeast in a small jug and stir in the warm water. Pour into the milk mixture. Add the lightly beaten egg, flaked almonds, raisins and chopped citron. Stir well.

Mix the flour, salt and cardamom in a basin. Make a well in the centre and pour in the liquid. Mix until all the ingredients are thoroughly combined. The dough will be quite sticky. Scrape the sides of the basin with a spatula and bring the dough into the centre. Pat gently to form a smooth round, and cover with a lightly oiled polythene bag. Set on top of a warm oven (or in a warm airing cupboard) for 2–3 hours. The dough should have almost doubled in bulk.

Turn the dough out onto a lightly floured surface and, dipping your hands occasionally into the bag of flour, knead for 7 minutes. The dough should now feel wet and heavy but not sticky. Have ready three oiled baking sheets. Divide the dough into three portions weighing about 1lb 3oz (530g). Work the portions into rounds, tucking the dough underneath itself so that the surface is smooth. Place on the baking sheets and cover with the polythene. Set in a warm, draught-free place for 45 minutes. Pre-heat the oven to 350°F (180°C), gas mark 4, and bake for 45 minutes.

For a shiny surface, brush with beaten egg after 20 minutes baking. Cool on a wire tray.

Soft cheeses

Introduction

Making cheese at home is just as simple as making bread. You do not need a cow in the back garden, a special dairy room or a ten-gallon bucket; but some background information may be useful.

Cheese is a curd. Unpasteurized milk will curd naturally over a certain period, as the milk's acidity is increased. Rennet can be added to make the milk curd more quickly.

The milk used for the recipes that follow is pasteurized. (I use the silver-topped milk delivered by the milkman.) Pasteurization not only kills harmful bacteria, but also kills bacteria which produce lactic acid. In order to make the milk curd naturally the lactic acid producing bacteria must be put back. This is known as adding a *starter*. You can buy a starter from certain laboratories, but this makes cheese-making rather complicated. The simplest alternative is to make your own starter (recipe on page 38), or use commercial buttermilk, which contains the correct bacteria. Another way to make the milk curd is to add an acid substance like orange juice or vinegar (recipes on pages 41 and 42).

So cheese-making is basically simple, but flavour and texture can be varied by alterations in the making of the cheese: by using whole or skimmed milk; adding more or less rennet; scalding the curd; heating the milk to a higher or lower temperature, etc.

Hygiene must be scrupulously observed in cheese-making. You will find the word 'sterilize' repeated several times in each recipe. Because milk is a perfect medium for the growth of harmful bacteria, all traces of it must be removed from utensils before they are used again.

This is how to sterilize utensils:
1. Rinse with cold water, scrub away traces of milk.
2. Wash in warm soapy water and rinse with cold water.
3. Fill the sink with cold water and add 2 tablespoons of household bleach. Immerse the utensils and swish them around for a few minutes.
4. Rinse them very thoroughly with cold water as any traces of bleach will spoil your cheese.

5. Leave utensils to drain until required. The drainer should be swilled with boiling water. Working surfaces must be wiped with bleach solution, then rinsed.

The dripping pole must be cleaned in the same way. (This is the pole from which cheese bags drip. I use a bamboo rod, but hooks, screwed into the bottom of wall cupboards, can also be used.)

Cheesecloth should always be boiled for 5 minutes before use. I buy the white dress-fabric cheesecloth. A large square, referred to in the recipes, is roughly 18in. (45cm) square. You should have five or six squares if you intend making many cheeses.

Wear an apron which covers as much of you as possible. Plastic ones are ideal because they can be wiped.

Try not to wear woollen clothing, as the tiny fibres always find their way into the cheese. If you have long hair, tie it back.

You will probably possess most of the necessary equipment, apart from a coulommiers mould. This, and small bottles of rennet and annatto (orange cheese colouring), can be bought from cheese equipment suppliers.

The largest quantity of milk used in the recipes is 7 pints (4 litres) so you will need a basin large enough to take this amount comfortably. You will also need a heavy-based pan for the same quantity. I use a pressure cooker pan. Basins can be of glass, plastic (unscratched), earthenware or stainless steel. 7 pints (or 4 litres) of milk make 1–1½lb (450–670g) of cheese.

I would advise using a jam-making thermometer rather than the dairy thermometer which is expensive and more fragile.

Rennet is measured in drops. A chemist may give you an empty bottle used for eye, nose or ear drops.

Wooden chopping boards and natural, undyed, straw place-mats are used for draining the cheeses.

The moulds used for the cheeses are round, loose-bottomed cake tins or cylindrical food cans with the tops and bottoms cut out.

The recommended storage time for each cheese is 1 week, but you will probably find that some of your

cheeses last a little longer. To keep the cheese, wrap it in cling film and store it in the fridge. To freeze it, wrap in cling film, then in foil. Put it in the 'fast freeze' compartment first. It should keep for 4 months. Yoghurt (page 44) does not freeze well.

Read through the recipes before you make any of the cheeses, in order to check that you have all the ingredients and necessary equipment.

Basic equipment for cheese-making

You will need: a large basin — it will be useful to have other basins and bowls of varying sizes; a jam-making (or candy) thermometer; long-handled spoon; fish slice; perforated spoon; long sharp knife; large heavy-based pan; natural straw place-mats (not dyed); wooden chopping boards; teacup; a knife, fork, teaspoon and tablespoon; an eye dropper; colander; squares of cheesecloth; soft, smooth string; a room thermometer hanging close to your working area.

Goat's milk cheese with a hint of brandy (or sherry), presented in a parcel of sweet chestnut leaves

Goat's milk cheese

7pt (4lt) unpasteurized goat's milk
4 tblsp buttermilk
16 drops cheese rennet
30–40 sweet chestnut leaves
10–12 tblsp liquor (e.g. rum, brandy, sherry)

Goat's milk can be bought from certain supermarkets, but you are more likely to find some at a local farm.

Boil a square of cheesecloth for 5 minutes. Sterilize a large basin, thermometer, tablespoon and eye dropper.

Pour the milk into the basin. Put the basin over a pan of boiling water and heat the milk to 90°F (32°C). Remove, stir in the buttermilk, add the rennet and mix thoroughly for 2 minutes. Cover with the cheesecloth and leave at room temperature 65°–75°F (18°–24°C), for 2 hours. The curd should be firm and smooth.

Meanwhile, prepare 2 cylindrical moulds (food cans) roughly 6in. (15cm) high and 4in. (10cm) diameter. Cut the base and top from the cans, then cut away the top and bottom ridges using a wall can-opener or scissors. The cans should be perfectly smooth inside — flatten any rough edges (with the back of an old spoon).

Re-boil the cheesecloth. Sterilize the cans, a straw mat, chopping board and perforated spoon. Put the board onto a sink drainer (previously swilled with boiling water), with the mat and cans on top.

Use the perforated spoon to transfer the curds to the cans. Hold the cans, otherwise the curds will slip out at the bottom. Cover with the cheesecloth, still holding down the cans, then quickly place a weight on top. Leave the cheeses to drain for 36–40 hours.

Sterilize a small measuring jug, a straw mat and a roasting tin. Stand the 2 cans of cheese on the mat, in the roasting tin. Measure the liquor into the jug (I use a mixture of anything we happen to have, rum, brandy or sherry) and pour slowly into the cheese cans. The liquor will drain out but some flavour will be absorbed by the cheeses. Pour the liquor back into the jug, then again over the cheese. Do this several times during the next 8 hours. Keep the cheeses and jug covered with clean cheesecloth.

Wash the chestnut leaves separately and dry between paper towels. Remove the cheeses from the cans and cover with leaves. Secure with soft string. Leave the cheeses to mature for 2 days before eating.

Lactic curd cheese

½ teacup milk
7pt (4lt) milk
½oz (14g) hard cheese (cheddar)

This is a lovely soft cheese which can be eaten as it is, flavoured (see lists of flavouring for yoghurt on page 44) or made into cheesecake.

Boil a small piece of cheesecloth for 5 minutes. Sterilize a teacup and thermometer. Heat the ½ teacup of milk to 95°F (35°C) by standing the cup in a pan of simmering water. Crumble the hard cheese into the milk. Cover with the cheesecloth and leave at room temperature, 65°–75°F (18°–24°C), for 24 hours. This is the *starter*.

Boil a square of cheesecloth for 5 minutes. Sterilize a large basin, thermometer and tablespoon.

Pour the 7pt (4lt) of milk into the basin. Put the basin over a pan of boiling water and heat the milk to 90°F (32°C). Mix in 4 tblsp of starter (the mixture in the cup which should now be solid). Cover the milk with the cheesecloth and leave at room temperature until the milk forms a jelly-like curd (up to 36 hours).

Boil 2 squares of cheesecloth and a length of string for 5 minutes. Sterilize a knife, colander, basin and the drip pole. Line the colander with the cloths and position over the basin. Break up the curds and pour some into the colander. Encourage drainage by gently scraping the bottom of the cloth. As the whey drains pour in the remaining curd. Bring the corners of the cloths together, tie with string and attach to the pole. Every 4 or 5 hours open the bag and scrape the curd into the centre. Let the bag drip for 20 hours. The cheese is now ready. (See pp.36–7 for storing and freezing. Save the whey and see page 42 for its uses.)

Basic recipe for cheesecake

Melt 3oz (85g) of butter in a pan. Mix in 8oz (225g) of crushed digestive biscuits. Turn into a round, loose-bottomed baking tin and refrigerate for 30 minutes. Beat 3 eggs in a basin until thick. Add one-quarter of the Lactic curd cheese; 8 tblsp double cream; the juice

The versatile Lactic curd cheese, ideal in cheesecakes

and grated rind of a lemon; ½ teasp vanilla essence and 8 tblsp sugar. Pour into the cake tin and bake for 1 hour at 350°F (180°C), gas mark 4. Turn the oven off, open the door and let the cake cool slowly.

Cream cheese

2pt (1.14lt) milk
1pt (570ml) top of milk
10 drops cheese rennet
2pt (1.14lt) single cream
1 tblsp buttermilk

These little cheeses are soft, easily spread and very creamy. They can be eaten plain, or flavoured (see yoghurt flavouring on page 45).

Boil a square cheesecloth for 5 minutes. Sterilize a large basin, thermometer, tablespoon and eye dropper.

Pour the milk, single cream and top of milk into the basin. (If you have not saved 'top of milk' substitute with 3 parts single cream and 1 part milk.) Put the basin into a sink of hot tap water. Slowly heat the milk to 70°F (21°C) by adding boiling water to the tap water. Remove the basin. Stir in the buttermilk, add the rennet and mix well for 2 minutes. To prevent all the cream from rising, stir the top of milk gently for five minutes. Repeat two or three times over the next hour. Cover with cheesecloth in between stirrings. The milk will take about 12 hours to curd; it should then

Cream cheese, delicious on crispy French bread

be like a soft jelly and come away from the sides of the basin when tipped slightly.

Boil 2 squares of cheesecloth and a length of string for 5 minutes. Sterilize a knife, colander, basin and the dripping pole. Line the colander with the cloths and position over the basin. Cut the curd into squares and pour a quarter of them into the colander. Encourage drainage by gently scraping the bottom of the cloth. As the whey drains, pour in the remaining curd. Bring the corners of the cloths together, tie with string and attach to the pole. Leave the bag to drip for 8 hours,

opening to scrape the curd into the centre twice during this time.

Sterilize a basin, fork, chopping board, straw mat and 5 little moulds, roughly 3in. (7cm) deep and 2in. (5cm) diameter (I use baby-food cans with the tops and bottoms cut out). Put the mat over the board and stand the moulds on top. Scrape the cheese into the basin and add salt to taste, also flavouring if desired. Press the cheese into the moulds. Cover and refrigerate for 2 hours. Remove from the the moulds. (See introduction on pp.36–7 for storing and freezing.)

Garlic and celery cheese

7pt (4lt) milk
6 tblsp wine vinegar
2oz (55g) celery seed
2 cloves garlic
1 teasp salt

These cheeses are similar to the French herb cheeses. Split a hot baked potato in half and let the cheese melt in the middle.

Boil a square cheesecloth and length of string for 5 minutes. Sterilize a large pan, long-handled spoon, colander, basin and the dripping pole.

Pour the milk into the pan. Stirring occasionally, bring it almost to boiling point. Remove from heat and add the vinegar. Stir well for a minute then let the curds settle for 15 minutes.

Line the colander with cheesecloth and place over the basin. Pour a quarter of the curd into the colander. Encourage drainage by gently scraping the bottom of the cloth. As the whey drains, slowly pour in the remaining curds. Bring the cheesecloth corners together, tie with string and tie to the pole. Leave the bag to drip for an hour.

Sterilize a basin, dish, fork and mortar and pestle. Pour the celery seeds into the dish. Crush the garlic cloves and salt into a paste. Turn the curds into the basin and add the garlic paste. Mix thoroughly. Put a piece of waxed paper on to kitchen scales and divide the cheese into 2oz (55g) portions: you should get seven or eight. Form the portions into balls and roll them in the celery seed. Put the balls between two pieces of waxed paper, cover with a bread board and press lightly. The cheese is now ready for eating but will keep for up to a week in the refrigerator. Cover with waxed paper or wrap in cling film.

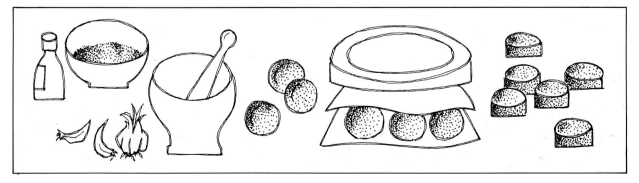

Citrus curd cheese

6 medium oranges
6 medium lemons
7pt (4lt) milk
salt to taste

This is a lovely, easily spread cheese with a definite hint of citrus fruit. My children love it. Try it on crisp squares of toast or biscuits. It is also ideal for sweet cheesecakes.

Boil 2 squares of cheesecloth (one large and one small) and a length of string, for 5 minutes.

Sterilize a large, heavy-based pan, a long-handled spoon, colander, basin and the dripping pole.

Scald a lemon squeezer and a jug. Cut the lemons and oranges in half, squeeze out the juice and strain into the jug through the small square of cheesecloth.

Pour the milk into the pan. Stirring occasionally, bring it almost to boiling point. Remove from heat and stir in the fruit juice. Leave the curds for 15 minutes while they settle.

Line the colander with the large cheesecloth and position over the basin. Pour a quarter of the curd into the colander. Encourage drainage by carefully scraping the bottom of the cloth. As the whey drains, slowly pour in the remaining curds. Bring the corners of the cheesecloth together, tie with string and tie to the pole. Leave the bag to drip for one hour.

Sterilize a basin and fork. Scrape the cheese from the cloth into the basin. Sprinkle with salt and mix.

The cheese is now ready to eat. It can be wrapped in cling film and refrigerated for up to a week. To freeze it, wrap in double cling film, then in foil.

A large quantity of whey will be left over after the cheese has been made. This can be put into sterilized milk bottles and refrigerated or put into sterilized yoghurt cartons, covered with foil and stored in the freezer. Whey makes a refreshing summer drink when served with ice and slices of lemon and orange; or heat it for a nourishing bedtime drink and add a teaspoon of honey. It can also be used in milk puddings, sweet pancakes, yorkshire puddings, biscuit or cake mixtures; or as a base for any of the white sauces.

Coulommiers cheese

3pt (1.7lt) milk
2 tblsp buttermilk
25 drops cheese rennet

A coulommiers mould consists of two small stainless steel hoops which fit into each other. They can be bought from cheese equipment suppliers, but if you have any difficulty getting them, please write to the publishers for advice.

Boil a square cheesecloth for 5 minutes. Sterilize a basin, thermometer, tablespoon and eye dropper.

Pour the milk into the basin. Put the basin over a pan of boiling water and heat the milk to 90°F (32°C). Remove from heat, stir in the buttermilk, add the rennet and mix thoroughly for 2 minutes.

Stir the top of the milk gently (to prevent all the cream from rising) until it thickens and begins to cling to the spoon. Cover with the cheesecloth and leave at room temperature 65°–75°F (18°–24°C) for 1–2 hours.

The curd should be firm and come away from the sides of the basin when tipped slightly. Re-boil the cheesecloth. Sterilize a coulommiers mould, a chopping board, straw mat and a perforated spoon. Put the board onto a sink drainer (previously swilled with boiling water), cover the board with the mat and position the mould on top.

Using a perforated spoon, very carefully transfer the curds to the moulds in thin slices. Allow the curds to drain for 30 minutes then cover with the cheesecloth. Leave at room temperature for 24 hours. The curd will shrink to half its original size.

Re-boil the cheesecloth. Sterilize another board and mat. Remove the top hoop, taking care not to move the lower hoop or the curd may slip out. Stand the mat and board on top of the lower hoop. Carefully turn the

whole thing over. Remove the used board and mat, wash and sterilize them immediately. Cover the curds with the cloth and leave to drain for a further 24 hours.

Repeat this process once or twice more. The cheese should be firm enough to stand without the mould.

Remove the mould and rub salt all over the surface of the cheese. Wrap it lightly in waxed paper and

Mild flavoured and smooth textured Coulommiers cheese

refrigerate for 24 hours before eating. The cheese will keep for a week wrapped in cling film, but you can cut out a wedge and freeze the remainder — see the instruction notes on pp.36–7.

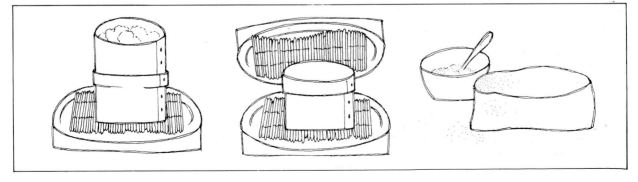

Yoghurt

2pt (1.14lt) milk
3 tblsp plain commercial yoghurt

This is much smoother and creamier than shop-bought yoghurt. (The commercial yoghurt is used as a starter.)

Place your room thermometer in the centre of the oven and switch on to the lowest mark. The temperature should fluctuate from 90°F (32°C) to 110°F (43°C). If it becomes hotter or cooler than these two degrees, adjust the switch accordingly.

Sterilize a basin, tablespoon, egg-beater and plate. Pour the milk into the basin and add the commercial yoghurt. Whisk thoroughly. Cover with the plate and put in the centre of the oven. Place the thermometer in front of the basin and check the oven temperature at intervals. The yoghurt will take about 6 hours to set. Remove the basin and carefully tip it to one side. The curd should be like a soft jelly and come away from the sides of the basin. Allow the yoghurt to cool, then refrigerate until required.

To make individual yoghurts, mix the milk and the commercial yoghurt in a sterilized jug, pour into sterilized plastic coffee cups or small jelly-moulds, cover and follow the above instructions.

It is rather difficult to flavour the yoghurt without disturbing the curd, but there are ways of flavouring without doing too much damage: carefully poke solid

Smooth and creamy home-made yoghurt

food into the yoghurt using a sterilized skewer; put food into the yoghurt (part of which is sticking above the surface) for a few hours and remove before eating; top the yoghurt with grated food or liquid.

Solid food flavour

Small fresh strawberries; stoned cherries; seedless grapes; diced pineapple; tangerine segments; cucumber; red and green peppers; smoked ham; Roquefort cheese; shrimps.

Infused flavour

Crushed liquorice or cinnamon stick, ginger root or vanilla pod; garlic clove; spring onion; smoked meat; sprig of mint or other fresh herbs.

Top flavouring

Grated chocolate; flaked almonds or coconut; clear honey; liqueur; rosehip or ginger syrup; crushed sweetmeal biscuits; grated cheddar cheese.

York cheese

5pt (2.84lt) and ¾pt (430ml) milk
1 tblsp and 1 teasp buttermilk
18 drops cheese rennet
1 teasp annatto

This cheese has an orange stripe through the centre.

Boil 2 square cheesecloths for 5 minutes. Sterilize a large and medium basin, thermometer, tablespoon, teaspoon and eye-dropper.

Pour the milk into the appropriate basins and heat both to 90°F (32°C) over pans of boiling water. Remove from heat. Take the large basin, stir in the tblsp of buttermilk, add 14 drops of rennet and mix thoroughly for 2 minutes. Cover with one of the cloths. Take the medium basin, stir in the teasp of buttermilk, add the annatto and mix well. Add 4 drops of rennet and mix well for 2 minutes. (It is important that the annatto is added before the rennet.) Cover with the other cloth and leave at room temperature 65°–75°F (18°–24°C) for 2–3 hours.

The curd should be smooth and jelly-like.

Prepare a square mould, roughly 8in. (20cm) deep and 4in. (10cm) across. I use a firm plastic container with the bottom cut out. Boil a cheesecloth. Sterilize a chopping board, straw mat, perforated spoon, plate, fish slice, small ladle and the mould.

Make an imprint with the mould into the surface of the white curd. Slice this out with the fish slice and slip it onto the plate. Cover with a clean plate.

Put the chopping board onto a swilled sink drainer, cover the board with the mat and put the mould on top. Using the perforated spoon, transfer the white curd to the mould and fill to the top (keep a firm grip on the mould). Cover with the cheesecloth and a heavy plate. Leave to drain for 45 minutes. The curds will have shrunk. Gently scoop up the whey on the cheese surface with the ladle. Spoon in all the orange curd. Cover and drain for 45 minutes. Scoop up the surface whey, then spoon in the remaining white curds. Slide the curd (from the plate) on top. Cover and drain for 36 hours. Remove the heavy plate after 4 hours. During draining, the board, mat and cloth should be replaced once. (See pp.36–7 for storing and freezing.)

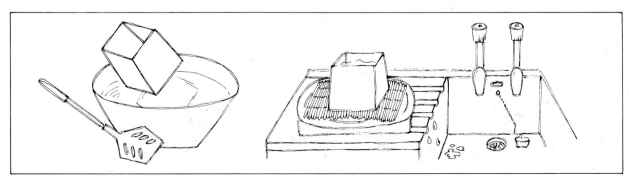

Chutneys, pickles and mustards

Introduction

One of the joys of preserving food is that the many jars of pickles, chutneys or relishes, complete with pretty covers and labels, can be shelved in a secluded corner and give a cosy farm-house atmosphere to a modern-style kitchen.

Most fruits and vegetables can be pickled or made into chutneys and relishes. It makes sense to have a preserving session when there is a glut and the food is relatively cheap. Vegetables and fruit should be in perfect condition when used for pickling, but bruises and imperfections can be cut away when making chutneys and relishes.

As pickles and chutneys are preserved in vinegar, it is important to remember that the vinegar is an acid which will corrode certain metals. Never use brass or copper pans. An aluminium preserving pan is fine for large quantities but should be well scoured before and after use. A stainless steel or unchipped enamel pan is also suitable. When bottling pickles, make sure that metal tops do not come into contact with vinegar. When cooking chutneys, use wooden spoons and never leave the mixture in a pan overnight.

Pickles are usually uncooked and left whole, or cut into neat pieces. Some vegetables are steeped in brine (salt water) for 24 hours before packing into jars. Do not pack the pickles to the top of the jar, leave about 1in. (2½cm) clear, then pour in the vinegar and fill almost to the brim — this will prevent the pickles at the top from becoming dry as the vinegar is absorbed. You will need small squares of muslin or cheesecloth to strain the spiced vinegar. To release any air bubbles, twist the jar sharply at intervals while filling. If some remain, poke very carefully into the jar with a knife, but try to avoid slicing the fruit or vegetables.

Many attractive preserving jars are available for pickles but ordinary jars can be used. To make an air-tight seal use clean cotton fabric dipped in paraffin wax. Secure with string or rubber bands.

Pickles are best left for about six weeks before eating. The only exception to this is pickled peppers which should be eaten within one month.

Chutneys are fruits or vegetables which are cooked for a long period on a low heat. The finished chutney should have a thick consistency with no excess liquid and no definable pieces of food.

A relish contains larger, recognizable pieces of food and is usually cooked for a shorter time.

To seal jars of chutney or relish you will need circles of waxed paper (I use the inner packets from boxes of cornflakes) and a block of paraffin wax, which can be bought from most chemists. Spoon the chutney into very clean, warm jars. Leave about ¾in. (2cm) clear at the top and cover immediately with a waxed paper circle. Leave until cold. Cut off a chunk of wax, place in a heat-proof jug and put the jug in a pan of water. Bring to the boil. When the wax has melted, pour into the jars and fill to the brim. When the wax has set hard, cover with circles of clear or coloured cellophane, paper doilies, pretty fabric or even thin wallpaper. Secure with strong rubber bands. Label, stating contents and date.

Chutneys and relishes improve if they are left to mature for at least two months.

Whole or ground spices are an important ingredient of pickles and chutneys. You will have a much better flavour if you grind your own each time you need them. I use a small coffee grinder, which is essential for the two mustards described on page 55.

Pickles and chutneys can accompany many savoury dishes — cold meats and continental sausages, salads, curries. My children like chutney spread liberally on

Spices are an essential ingredient of preserved foods

wholewheat bread, with chunks of crumbly Cheshire cheese. Corn relish makes an unusual filling for fluffy omelettes or pancakes.

Basic equipment:

For pickles: a large basin for brine; small basin for pickling spices; cooking pan; sharp vegetable knife; two tea towels; perforated spoon; preserving jars (each recipe indicates whether small, medium or large); measuring jug; pieces of muslin for straining the spices; adhesive labels.

For chutneys: a sharp vegetable knife; large heavy-based pan (aluminium is best, never use brass or copper); wooden spoon; clean jars; waxed paper; paraffin wax (available from most chemists); jar covers; strong rubber bands; adhesive labels.

For the mustards: a basin; wooden spoon; small coffee grinder; screw-topped jars; labels.

Sweet piccalilli

1 small cauliflower, ½ cucumber, ½ small marrow
½lb (220g) each of pickling onions,
    French beans and green tomatoes
7 tblsp cooking salt
3½pt (2lt) cold water
3 dried chillis, 3 bay leaves, 12 allspice
1½pt (850ml) white malt vinegar
2 tblsp cornflour
3 teasp each of tumeric and dry mustard
2 teasp ground ginger
10 tblsp soft brown sugar

Wash the cauliflower and cut into small flowerettes. Peel the onions. Wash the beans and cut into 1in. (2½cm) lengths. Wash the tomatoes and cut into quarters. Wash the cucumber and marrow; cut them into neat pieces.

Pour the water into a large basin, add the cooking salt and stir until it dissolves. Put the prepared vegetables into the brine, then put a plate on top to keep them submerged. Cover with a clean tea towel and leave for 48 hours.

Put the cornflour, tumeric, mustard, ginger and sugar into a basin and mix to a cream with a little of the vinegar. Put the remaining vinegar in a large pan.

Add the chillis, bay leaves and allspice. Bring to the boil, and boil for 15 minutes.

Drain the vegetables and rinse thoroughly with cold water. Remove the spices from the vinegar using a perforated spoon. Add the vegetables, bring to the boil, and boil for 5 minutes.

Drain the vinegar into the creamed cornflour. Mix well. Pour the sauce over the vegetables, stir and cook gently for 10 minutes.

Spoon the piccalilli into clean warm jars and cover with circles of waxed paper. Leave until cold. Seal and label. Keep for two months before eating.
Yield: 4½lb (2kg).

If you prefer hot piccalilli, use the same vegetables and the same amount of vinegar but increase the sauce ingredients and the spices.

Mix the following to a cream with some of the vinegar: 5 teasp tumeric, 4 teasp dry mustard, 3 teasp cayenne pepper, 6 tblsp ground ginger, 6 tblsp soft brown sugar and 2 tblsp cornflour.

Pour the remaining vinegar into a large pan and add: 7 dried chillis, 3 bay leaves, 12 allspice, 12 black and 12 white peppercorns.

Bring to the boil, and boil for 15 minutes. Follow the remaining recipe given for sweet piccalilli.

Pickled onions

2lb (0.9kg) pickling onions
1pt (570ml) cold water
2 tblsp cooking salt
approx ½pt (280ml) white malt vinegar
10 allspice and 10 cloves
2 bay leaves
1 teasp broken mace
3in. (8cm) stick cinnamon
piece root ginger

Pour the water into a large basin, add the salt, and stir until dissolved. Peel the onions. Put them into the brine with a plate on top to keep them submerged. Cover with a clean cloth and leave for 24 hours.

Put the vinegar and spices (break up the cinnamon and bruise or break the root ginger) into a basin over a pan of water. Bring the water to the boil, and boil for 5 minutes. Remove the basin and cover with a clean cloth. Leave the spices to steep for two hours.

Drain the onions and rinse them in cold water. Pack them into a large clean preserving jar, leaving 1in. (2½cm) clear at the top. Strain the vinegar and pour it over the onions. Twist the jar sharply at intervals to release air bubbles. Fill to the top, secure the lid, and label. Keep for six weeks before eating.

Pickled eggs

15 pullet's or small chicken eggs
1pt (570ml) white wine vinegar
a little salt
1 tblsp fresh sage leaves
1 tblsp fresh thyme leaves

If the sage and thyme have just been picked from the garden, wash them thoroughly in cold water to remove traces of greenfly etc.

Put the herbs and vinegar into a basin over a pan of water, and boil for 5 minutes. Remove the basin and cover with a clean cloth. Leave the herbs to steep in the warm vinegar for two hours.

Have the eggs at room temperature for at least an hour before boiling. Place them in a pan and cover with cold water. Add some salt to seal the shells. Bring to the boil, and boil for 15 minutes, stirring occasionally to keep the yolks in the centre.

Plunge the eggs into cold water. Remove shells and skins. Pack into a clean, medium-sized preserving jar leaving about 1in. (2½cm) clear at the top. Strain the vinegar, squeezing juices from the herbs, and pour into the jar. Twist it sharply at intervals to release air bubbles. Fill to the top, secure the lid and attach a label. Do not keep for more than two months.

Pickled mushrooms

2lb (0.9kg) button mushrooms
½pt (280ml) white malt vinegar
juice of 3 lemons
1 teasp cooking salt
½pt (280ml) cold water
two 3in. (8cm) sticks cinnamon
12 cloves

Put the broken cinnamon sticks, cloves and vinegar into a basin over a pan of water. Bring the water to boil, and boil for 5 minutes. Remove the basin, cover with a cloth and leave for two hours.

Put the mushrooms in cold water and gently remove any soil or compost. Trim away ragged stalks.

Put the water, lemon juice and salt in a pan and bring to the boil. Plunge six or seven mushrooms into the water. Leave them for no longer than 2 minutes. Remove with a perforated spoon and drain on paper towels. Continue this process until all the mushrooms have been blanched.

Pack the mushrooms into 2 small, clean preserving jars with the stalks facing inwards. Leave 1in. (2½cm) clear at the top. Strain the vinegar through muslin and pour over the mushrooms, twisting the jar to release air bubbles. Fill to the top, secure the lids, and label. Keep for six weeks before eating.

Pickled beetroot

1¾lb (780g) beetroot
½pt (280ml) white malt vinegar
1 teasp coriander
12 allspice
6 black peppercorns
1 dried chilli

Put the spices and vinegar into a basin over a pan of cold water. Bring the water to boil, and boil for 5 minutes. Remove the basin, cover with a clean tea towel and leave the spices to steep in the warm vinegar for about 2 hours.

Wash the beetroots carefully in cold water. Put them in a pan and just cover with salted water. Bring to the boil, then simmer until tender, about 1½ hours.

Drain the beetroots and leave until cold. Carefully peel away the skins and cut into neat ½in. (1½cm) cubes or ½in. (1cm) slices.

Pack the beetroot carefully into two small, clean preserving jars. Strain the vinegar through muslin into a jug. Pour over the beetroot, twisting the jar at intervals to release air bubbles (if some bubbles remain, poke a knife into the jar to release them but try to avoid cutting the beetroot). Fill to the top, secure the lids, and attach labels. Keep the beetroot for at least six weeks before eating.

Pickled vegetables

1 small cauliflower
½lb (220g) each of French beans,
   pickling onions and green tomatoes
½ cucumber, ½ marrow
3½pt (2lt) cold water
7 tblsp cooking salt
approx. 1½pt (850ml) white malt vinegar
8 white peppercorns
1 teasp each of cloves and coriander
6 cloves garlic, finely sliced

Wash the cauliflower and cut into flowerettes. Wash
the beans and cut into 1in. (2cm) lengths. Peel the
onions. Wash the tomatoes and cut into quarters.
Wash the cucumber and marrow and cut into neat

Vegetables are steeped in brine before bottling

pieces. Put the vegetables in a large pan and cover with
brine (the salt dissolved in the water). Put a plate on
top to keep them submerged. Cover with a clean tea-
towel and leave for 24 hours.

Put the vinegar, spices and garlic into a basin over a
pan of water. Bring the water to boil, and boil for 5
minutes. Remove the basin, cover with a tea-towel,
and leave the spices to steep for 2 hours.

Drain the vegetables and rinse in cold water. Pack
into 3 clean, medium-sized preserving jars. Leave 1in.
(2½cm) clear at the top. Strain the vinegar and pour
over the vegetables. Twist the jar at intervals to release
air bubbles. Fill it to the top, secure the lids, and label.
Keep for six weeks before eating.

Pickled orange slices

5 firm oranges
approx. ¾pt (430ml) white malt vinegar
1lb (450g) granulated sugar
8 each of cardamom pods, cloves and allspice
5in. (12cm) stick cinnamon
2 teasp broken mace

Wash the oranges thoroughly. Prick them with a clean sewing needle to prevent shrinkage. Put them in a pan and cover with water. (Put a plate on the oranges to keep them submerged.) Bring to the boil, then cover and simmer gently for 40 minutes.

Remove the oranges and plunge them into cold water to cool rapidly. Keep 10 tblsp of the water. Cut the oranges into ½in. (1cm) slices. Put the vinegar, water and sugar into a large pan. Put the spices (break

Pickled orange slices — a treat for the Christmas table

up the cardamom and cinnamon) into a muslin bag and add it to the pan. Simmer and stir until the sugar dissolves. Add the orange slices, and simmer for 30 minutes.

Lift the slices into a basin. Add the spice bag and syrup. Keep the slices submerged with a plate. Cover with a cloth and leave for 10 hours.

Pack the slices into a large, clean preserving jar, leaving 1in. (2½cm) clear at the top. Boil the syrup and the spices for 10 minutes, then pour the syrup over the slices, and twist the jar at intervals to release air bubbles. Fill it to the top. Leave until cold. Secure the lid, and attach a label. Keep for six weeks before eating.

54

Pickled cherries

1½lb (670g) Morello cherries
1pt (570ml) red wine vinegar
¾lb (340g) granulated sugar
3 teasp aniseed and 4 cloves
2in. (5cm) stick cinnamon
1in. (2½cm) root ginger

Pour the vinegar into a pan with the sugar. Break the cinnamon into small pieces and bruise the ginger root. Add them, with the aniseed and cloves, to the vinegar. Bring to the boil, then simmer, stirring continually until the sugar has dissolved. Remove from heat and cover the pan with a clean cloth. Leave the spices to steep in the warm vinegar for 2 hours.

Sort the cherries, discarding any which are bruised or blemished, and remove the stalks. Wash the cherries in cold water. (The stones can also be removed, but this tends to leave the cherries in rather a messy state.) Pack them into 2 clean, medium-sized preserving jars, leaving about 1in. (2½cm) clear at the top.

Strain the vinegar through muslin into the jars, twisting the jars sharply at intervals to release air bubbles. Fill them to the top, secure the lids, and attach labels. Keep for six weeks before eating.

Pickled pineapple

Two 1lb (450g) tins pineapple cubes
approx. 1pt (570ml) cider vinegar
10 cloves
1 teasp cooking salt
1 teasp mustard seed
2 cloves garlic
1 piece root ginger

Peel and slice the garlic. Bruise or break the root ginger. Put the salt, spices, garlic and vinegar into a basin over a pan of water. Bring the water to boil, and boil for 5 minutes. Remove the basin and cover it with a clean tea towel. Leave the spices to steep in the warm vinegar for 2 hours.

Drain the pineapple cubes. (Refrigerate the juice and use it as a cool summer drink or as a base for fruit salad.) Pack the cubes into two small, clean preserving jars leaving 1in. (2½cm) clear at the top.

Strain the vinegar through muslin into a jug and pour it over the pineapple. Twist the jar sharply at intervals to release any air bubbles. (If some air bubbles remain, carefully poke into the jar with a knife to release them.) Fill to the top, secure the lids, and attach labels. Keep for six weeks before eating.

Hot mustard

4 tblsp mustard seed
4 dried chillis
12 black and 12 white peppercorns
12 cloves and 12 allspice
1 teasp coriander
1 teasp each of cayenne pepper, turmeric
    and ground ginger
1 teasp paprika pepper
1 teasp cooking salt
16 tblsp white wine vinegar

Grind the mustard seed a tablespoon at a time. Grind the first tablespoon very coarsely so that some of the seeds remain whole; grind the second less coarsely; the third still less and the fourth to a powder. Put the seeds into a basin. Split the chillis, extract the seeds and grind roughly. (Keep the pods for soups, stews etc.) Roughly grind the peppercorns, allspice, cloves and coriander. Add these to the mustard.

Add the cayenne and paprika peppers, the turmeric, ginger and salt. Mix thoroughly.

Add the vinegar two tablespoons at a time and mix after each addition. The mustard should be wet, with a little excess liquid, but not runny. Transfer to clean jars with plastic screw tops. Fill to the brim, and secure the tops as tightly as possible. Label. Keep for one month before eating.

Sweet cardamom mustard

4 tblsp mustard seed
12 black and 6 white peppercorns
6 cloves
1 teasp aniseed
1 teasp dried mint
12 cardamom pods
1 teasp grated nutmeg
6 teasp paprika pepper
2 tblsp soft brown sugar
14 tblsp red wine vinegar

Grind the mustard seed a tablespoon at a time. Grind the first tablespoon very coarsely so that some of the seed remains whole; grind the second less coarsely; the third still less and the fourth to a powder. Put the seeds into a basin.

Add the roughly ground black and white peppercorns, cloves, aniseed and mint. Split the cardamom pods, extract the seeds, grind them almost to a powder and add them to the basin with the grated nutmeg, paprika pepper and sugar. Mix thoroughly.

Add the vinegar two tablespoons at a time and mix after each addition. The mustard should be wet, with a little excess liquid, but not runny. Transfer to clean jars with plastic screw tops. Fill to the brim and secure the tops as tightly as possible. Label. Keep for one month before eating.

Recipes

The recipes that follow ignore the possibility that the smoker may have fish which he has caught himself, or freshly killed pork that needs attention. It is assumed that the weather will be dry, since wet, muggy weather delays the drying process. The temptation to raise the temperature of smoke production to speed drying in wet weather must be resisted. The remedy lies in patiently extending the time allowed for gentle smoke drying, with the fire kept low as always, even if this means the fire pit must be cleaned out and a fresh start made to keep up the output of smoke.

When the urge to cure and smoke diminishes, give it a rest. When it returns, clean out the holes, or dig new ones, and try again. The method is sound and natural. No outside source of energy is used. It is genuine smoke-curing, true to the age-old traditions, but brought up to date for use at home.

Buckling

If herrings are packed like sardines, each layer covered with salt, enough liquid is drawn out to cover them in saturated brine, and in this condition they can be kept for considerable periods so long as the temperature is maintained around freezing point. Such herrings are used for making buckling. The head is cut off, and the gut withdrawn, the excess salt being soaked out in fresh water. They are hung on the hook two at a time, the point being inserted in the flesh close to the tail fin. After smoke-drying for 8 hours, they are cooked for 2 hours, the smoker being made up with charcoal. The flesh is more consolidated than with bloaters, and they are packed after smoking compressed together. They will keep for some time in the refrigerator, and make a useful, ready-to-eat snack, or an additional item for the hors d'oeuvres tray.

61

Bloaters

One of the tastiest common herring products is the bloater. It is a fresh herring caught when containing roe, brined and smoke-dried. Brining time is 2–3 hours, even longer for a big oily fish. It can be gutted before or after soaking, its unusable innards being pulled out through a cut made in the 'throat' by nipping them between the back of the knife and the cutting board, and drawing the fish away. Smoke drying takes about 8 hours. The cooking at the end is minimal, a mere 30 minutes or so, with the damper board taken away.

The craftsman's way of spitting bloaters is to press the head to one side so as to open a gap between the body and the gill case. A pointed stick is introduced into the opening and pushed out through the mouth. The operation is repeated, all the fish being kept the same way round. Sharpened bloater spits made of ½in. (13mm) dowel will be worth making if bloaters are to be done regularly. Alternatively, they can be hooked up, two per hook, the point being pushed in just below the head in the centre of the back.

The bloaters can be kept up to five days hanging in the litter-type box, or somewhat longer in the refrigerator. They are gashed twice and grilled five minutes on each side.

Bloaters, one of the tastiest herring products

Kippers

The other popular cured-herring product is the kipper. This is split open before it is smoked. The fish is laid flat on the cutting board, head to the left, and held (by right-handed people) with the left hand. The fish's back is towards the operator. He inserts the point of the knife, cutting edge to the left, just where the head begins and cuts it in two, leaving a 'cheek' and eye in each half, keeping the knife horizontal. Then, turning the knife round, he cuts towards the tail. But the point of the knife is kept short of penetrating much beyond the backbone, otherwise the result would be two fillets instead of one kipper. The herring is opened and the gills, gut and roe removed, the roe being kept for separate use. The fish is washed, and put in brine for 1 hour. It is rinsed again, and hung on a hook so that it is held open.

The smoking time is 8 hours, with enough cooking at the end merely to ensure that it finishes dry. Kippers should be kept like bloaters, but remember that once opened, they will tend to dry up sooner. The colour of kippers shows a marked contrast to the factory product which is dyed dark brown, while the natural colour is slightly straw-coloured.

Kippers are commonly grilled, but they are equally delicious, and often considered more digestible, if stood in a jug which is then filled with boiling water from the kettle. They are ready in a matter of a few minutes.

Kippering was invented by a Northumberland fish curer, John Woodger, in about 1843.

Sprats

Smoked sprats are done like bloaters. Spitting on ³/₁₆in. (10mm) dowels, sharpened at one end, involves bending the fish head to one side, inserting the spit between the body and the gill case and pushing it out through the mouth. It is difficult at first, but speed develops with practice. Brining takes 1–3 hours, depending on size and oil content. Smoke drying requires 4 hours, and brief cooking finishes them off. They need only a short period in extra heat, and should look more silver than golden when done. They can be tested by your seeing if the flesh comes cleanly off the bone. The spits can be laid across the open smoke pit. The fish need no gutting and are eaten without a knife or fork, usually picked up by the head and tail and bitten in the back. They can be served the day after smoking.

Rainbow trout

If the trout needs to be purchased, the gilled and gutted packs of rainbow trout consisting of graded 8oz (220g) fish are recommended. Otherwise, if whole round trout are the alternative, the gills are pulled out with the gut, and the fish washed. The mackerel recipe (page 64) covers the rest of the process, except that the times given should be reduced by about one-third.

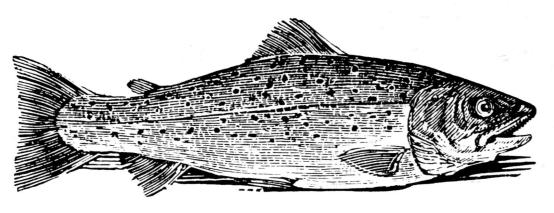

Sweets

Introduction

When you produce, in your own kitchen, the same mouth-watering and exotic sweets which line the shelves of a confectioner's, there is a real sense of achievement, not to say amazement. One of the results which surprised me after my first attempt was barley sugar. This is a subtly flavoured sweet and I was doubtful whether the flavour could be successfully recreated. But the process was simple and the results perfect.

One of the secrets of making sweets which require sugar boiling is to cover the pan with a lid for a minute or two so that the steam can wash down any crystals. This will prevent the mixture from turning into a thick grainy mass. (The only exception is the butter-mint recipe on page 79 which needs to be turned into a 'grainy mass' so as to produce little rock formations.)

Children can be included in a session of sweet-making, but it is advisable not to involve them in the cooking stages, since boiling sugar can give a nasty and painful scald. My children enjoy tossing the marshmallows in icing sugar, stuffing the dates with almond paste, rolling the apricot leather and twisting the barley sugar. (You must expect to have a slightly diminished selection by the time they have finished — it is amazing how many 'mis-shapes' they find!)

Equipment

The two most important pieces of equipment needed for sweet-making are a large heavy-based pan and a candy thermometer. The temperature of sugar can be tested by dropping some of the syrup into cold water,

but this method is not very accurate and it can cause the sweets to be too brittle or too soft.

Other necessary equipment: measuring spoons; pallet knife; wooden spoon; teaspoon; sharp pointed knife; heat-proof basins; baking tins; wire cooling tray.

Storing

Most of the sweets in this chapter will keep for a week or two if carefully stored. The sweets can be individually wrapped in cling film and stored in a polythene bag, or they can be arranged on layers of waxed paper (the inside packets from cornflakes boxes are suitable) and stored in an airtight jar or box. Sweets which have been tossed in icing sugar should have extra sugar sprinkled between the layers.

Home-made sweets and candies make charming gifts for birthday and Christmas. Many stationers sell fluted paper sweet cases and decorative boxes which make ideal containers. Different coloured cellophanes are also available. These can be made to resemble straw by cutting into fine strips — cover the top layer of sweets with a handful, before securing the lid. The cellophane can also be used to wrap individual sweets.

Freezing

When making large quantities of sweets, it is best to freeze some of them and so preserve flavour and colour. Wrap each sweet individually in cling film and place it in a polythene bag or rigid container. They will keep for up to 2 months. Thaw for 1 hour before eating. Some will need re-dusting with icing sugar.

*Almond paste fruits, Apricot leather rolls and Chewy
treacle toffee. The recipes for these are on page 72*

Turkish delight

4 tblsp gelatine powder
1pt (570ml) water
2lb (900g) granulated sugar
2 tblsp rose water
1 teasp red food colour
4 tblsp icing sugar
2 tblsp cornflour

Lightly oil an 8in. (20cm) square baking tin. Put the water, gelatine and sugar in a heavy-based pan. Heat gently and stir until the sugar dissolves. Bring to the boil and simmer for 25 minutes. Remove from heat and stir in the rose water and colour. Leave for 15 minutes. Lay a piece of paper towel on the mixture,

Turkish delight, Orange nut drops and Barley sugar

then lift it off (this will remove the cloudy surface). Pour the mixture into the baking tin and leave in a cool place for 24 hours. Mix the cornflour and icing sugar together, sprinkle some on a working surface and dust a sharp knife. Loosen the edges of the mixture with the knife, then pull up one of the corners and peel out onto the working surface. Cut into 8 strips, then cut each strip into 8 cubes. Toss each cube in the sugar and flour mixture. To store, arrange on layers of waxed paper (the inner packet from a cornflakes box is ideal) in an airtight box or jar, sprinkling the cornflour and icing sugar between each layer. To freeze, wrap each cube in cling film and place in a rigid container.

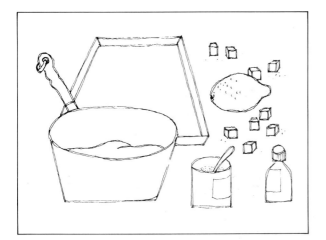

Barley sugar

12 sugar cubes
1 lemon
1lb (450g) granulated sugar
½pt (280ml) water
pinch of cream of tartar
6 drops yellow food colour

These ingredients make about 40 barley sugar twists. Oil a shallow baking tin, 8 × 12in. (20 × 30cm). Rub the sugar cubes over the lemon to absorb some of the essential oils. Put the cubes, granulated sugar and water in a heavy-based pan. Simmer and stir until the sugar dissolves. Add the cream of tartar and bring to the boil. Boil to 245°F (118°C). Cut the lemon in half, squeeze out the juice and add it to the pan. Boil to 300°F (148°C). Remove from heat and stir in the yellow food colour. When the bubbles subside, pour the mixture into the baking tin. After about 4 minutes, mark the candy into narrow strips using an oiled knife. Put the tin on top of a warm oven — you will have to work quickly at this point — pull the strips out of the tin. Cut them in half with oiled scissors. Twist the strips and leave them on an oiled working surface until set. Store wrapped in waxed paper or cling film. See page 70 for freezing.

Orange nut drops

4 oranges
10 tblsp evaporated milk
1½lb (670g) granulated sugar
pinch of salt
6oz (170g) chopped mixed nuts
2 tblsp icing sugar
2 tblsp cornflour

The ingredients given here make about 100 drops. Grate the oranges finely, cut them in half and squeeze out the juice. Put 6 tablespoons of the juice in a small pan and simmer on a low heat. Heat the evaporated milk in a basin over a pan of simmering water. Put 8oz (220g) of the sugar in a heavy-based pan and melt, on a medium heat, until brown. Reduce the heat and stir in the hot orange juice and milk, the remaining sugar and the salt. Stir until the sugar dissolves. Increase the heat and boil to 240°F (115°C). Remove from heat, stir in the orange peel and chopped nuts. Stir for 5 minutes. Then, using a teaspoon, drop the mixture onto a generously oiled working surface. After 15 minutes dust both hands with the mixed icing sugar and cornflour and roll each blob into a ball. Leave for about 6 hours before wrapping. See page 70 for storing and freezing.

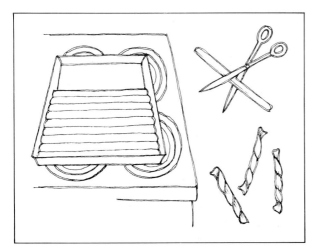

Nature's drinks

Introduction

Many of the drinks described in this chapter are made from easily obtainable berries, nuts, roots, leaves and flowers. Gathering the 'fruits of the earth' on a clear autumn day in the countryside, and then returning home to preserve their flavour, is much more lastingly enjoyable than buying manufactured 'soft drinks' and fizzy lemonade.

These drinks are easy to make, although some preparation time is required, and patience is needed to destalk elderberries and chop rosehips. But the result is worthwhile: bottles of wholesome drinks with no artificial flavouring, colouring or preservatives, at a fraction of the price of commercial drinks.

Sterilization. Processing and Waxing are mentioned in some of the recipes, for they comprise a sterilization method which ensures that the bottles are airtight. All bottles should be washed with soap and water, boiled for 5 minutes, then placed in a warm oven until they are needed. Boil their plastic screw-tops for at least 15 minutes before use. When the juice is ready for bottling, fill the bottles to within 1in. (25mm) of the top and screw the cap on tightly. Place a tea-towel in the bottom of a pan. Stand the bottles on top of this and fill with water up to the level of juice. Fold another tea-towel length-wise and weave this between the bottles so they do not bang against one another (if there is enough space in the pan for the bottles to fall, fill the gap with empty ones). Boil for 15 minutes. Remove and allow to cool. Meanwhile, put a chunk of paraffin wax in a basin and stand this in a pan of boiling water. When the bottles are cold, submerge the tops in the melted wax. The jug used for pouring juice into bottles should be heat-resistant. Always scald it with boiling water just before using.

When straining juices, use a square piece of muslin and a stool. Turn the stool upside down, position a basin to catch the juices, and tie each corner of the material to a stool leg. Use flannelette to strain rosehips; it is thicker than muslin and stops the harmful hip-hairs getting into the juice.

A liquidiser is very useful for many of the recipes, but it is not essential. You can buy the spices needed for some recipes in health-food shops. Chemists usually sell paraffin wax.

Finishing touches: when you serve iced or chilled drinks, dip the rims of glasses into egg white, then into caster sugar and leave to dry. To make ice cubes for fruit drinks, half fill the cube tray with water, add a piece of fruit or mint leaf, then freeze. Top up the tray and freeze again. Do not forget that a little grated nutmeg adds a spicy fragrance to hot drinks.

Essential equipment for home-made drinks

You will need: glass bottles with plastic screw-tops; various-sized basins and bowls; a heavy-based pan; teaspoons; tablespoons, wooden spoons; potato masher; heat resistant jug; a stool; large squares of muslin and flannelette; two tea-towels; a liquidizer (an alternative would be to use a mincer or, failing that, a sharp knife with plenty of elbow grease!)

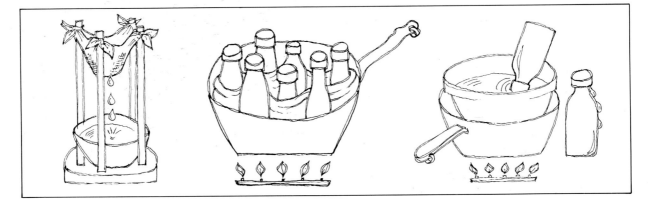

Blackberry cordial: blackberries are steeped in wine
vinegar and left for 7 days in an earthenware jar

Blackberry cordial

Place 4lb (1.8kg) of freshly picked blackberries in an earthenware jar. Cover with 35fl.oz (1lt) of white wine vinegar. Leave for 7 days, mashing twice daily to extract the juices. Alternatively, put the fruit and vinegar through a liquidizer and leave in the jar for 3 days, stirring occasionally.

Pour the purée into muslin and strain the juice into a pan. Place the pan on a low heat and add 2lbs (895g) of sugar and 1lb (445g) of clover honey. Stir until the sugar dissolves, bring to the boil, and simmer for 1 hour. Strain again to remove the scum. Bottle, process and wax.

The cordial is best diluted and can be taken as a hot tonic for colds, or as an iced summer drink.

Rose petal tea

You can use any really fragrant roses, although the old-fashioned dark red ones have the strongest scent. The aromatic quality of rose petals increases as they lose their moisture, so a finer flavour is obtained by drying them first. Gather the roses (almost fully open) early in the morning. Remove the petals and cut away the colourless base. Place on an open-weave cloth in an airing cupboard. The petals are dry when they are hard, but do not shatter when touched. Store in an airtight jar away from direct sunlight.

Allow 1 level tablespoon of petals to 1 cup. Pour over boiling water and steep for 7 minutes. Serve in an elegant glass with two fresh petals floating on the tea (they are edible).

Dandelion root coffee

This has a bitter-sweet flavour. It can be used alone or blended with ground coffee beans.

The roots may be dug up at any time of the year. Choose straight ones, as it is difficult to get the fat, gnarled ones perfectly clean. You can wash the dandelion leaves and use them in a salad; they are highly nutritious.

Scrub the roots well. Place them on a pan, just cover with water, and boil. Strain, and lay them on a piece of kitchen roll. When the excess moisture has been absorbed chop the roots to the size of coffee beans. Scatter them on a clean baking sheet and roast in a medium-hot oven for 1½ hours. Grind the coffee and allow 2 tblsp per 1pt (½lt) of water.

Ginger syrup

Put ½lb (225g) of root ginger into a basin, cover it with cold water and leave to soak overnight. Slice the ginger as finely as possible or put it through a liquidizer. Put it in a heavy pan and add 1pt (560ml) of cold water, 2lbs (895g) of sugar, and half a stick of cinnamon. Stir over a low heat until the sugar has dissolved. Put a lid on the pan and cook gently for an hour. Strain the ginger through muslin. Pour the juice into small bottles, process and wax.

Ginger syrup can be used in many delicious ways. Pour it over milk pudding, ice cream, fruit salad or steamed pudding; add a teaspoonful when making lime jelly; and make a tangy drink using iced water, a tablespoon of syrup and the juice of an orange.

Tomato juice

Remove the stalks from and wash 4lb (1.8kg) of tomatoes. Cut them into small pieces, place in a heavy pan and cover with 10fl.oz (285ml) of cold water. Put on a low heat and simmer, pressing the tomatoes into the sides of the pan with a wooden spoon. When they are soft, rub them through a fine sieve (or put them through a liquidizer). Pour the purée into a piece of muslin and squeeze gently to extract the juices.

Pour the juice into a pan, add a tablespoon of sugar, a teaspoon of salt and a little freshly ground black pepper. Bring slowly to the boil. Pour into hot bottles, process and wax.

Serve chilled with ice cubes, and with a dash of Worcestershire sauce.

Camomile tea

Camomile tea has been recorded as a medicinal herbal drink since the fifteenth century. Nicholas Culpeper (1616–1654) wrote: 'A decoction made of camomile, and drank, taketh away all pains and stitches in the side . . . it comforteth all parts that have need of warmth, digesteth and dissolveth whatsoever hath need thereof, by a wonderful speedy property'.

Camomile grows wild in areas of Britain, particularly on grassy and heathy parts in the milder south. Two varieties are the Roman and the German. The Roman is used to make sweet-scented lawns, the German is cultivated for medicinal use, though both can be used for teas.

The tea is often taken as a night-cap to aid

relaxation. Use a heaped teaspoon of dried flower-heads per cup and make as for normal tea. Brew for 8 minutes.

Rose petal tea: the most fragrant petals used for this delicate tea belong to the old-fashioned dark, red rose. The petals increase their perfume as they dry

Lavender & lime flower tea

Lavender and lime flower tea, recommended as a calming drink for nervous and tense people

Cut the flowering spikes of lavender from July onwards. Tie them in bundles and hang them in an airing cupboard for 4–5 days.

After the drying period, run two fingers down each spike and let the dried flowers fall into a screw-topped jar. Secure the lid and store in a cupboard or away from direct sunlight.

The tall lime (linden) tree can sometimes be found wild, but is usually grown to form avenues in parks or playing fields. The yellow flowers bloom in July and hang in scented clusters. Dry them flat on a piece of open-weave material in the airing cupboard for about

2 weeks. Store as for lavender. (If you have any difficulty in finding the linden tree, dried lime flowers can be bought from some herbalists.)

When making the tea, allow 1 level tablespoon of both lavender and lime for 2 cups. Cover with the boiling water and leave the flowers to steep for 5–8 minutes. Strain, and sweeten, if desired, with a teaspoon of clear honey.

Lime and lemon barley water

This drink has a slightly bitter tang. Serve as a summer drink with crushed ice and thin slices of lime and lemon.

Put 8oz (225g) of pearl barley in a large pan, and just cover with water. Bring to the boil, and then drain. Pour 3½pt (2.5lt) of cold water over the barley and put on a low heat. Chop 5 lemons and 5 limes into small pieces (or put them in a liquidizer) and add to the barley. Bring to the boil, then leave to simmer gently on a low heat for 1 hour.

Pour the pulp into a square of muslin (see page 80) and leave the juices to drip. The bag may be squeezed

Lime and lemon barley water, one of the most refreshing summer drinks, especially after a game of tennis!

gently to encourage the thick barley sediment through the cloth. Pour the juices into a pan and place on a low heat. Add 10oz (280g) of granulated sugar and stir until it dissolves. Remove from heat and leave to cool. Pour into bottles and refrigerate. Dilute to taste. Larger quantities of the barley water should be processed and waxed (see page 80).

85

Spiced nettle tea, enthusiastically recommended by most herbalists as a cure for many ailments

Spiced nettle tea

Nettle tea has been used as a medicinal drink for centuries. It has been recommended for warding off colds, soothing sore throats, toning up the arteries, and easing obesity and many other ailments.

Wearing gloves, pick the young, bright green leaves at the top of each plant. Wash the nettles under cold running water and shake in a colander to dry. Weigh 6oz (170g) of nettles and place in a pan. Cover with 35fl.oz (1lt) of cold water. Add ½ stick of cinnamon, grated nutmeg, a small piece of root ginger, 4 cardamon pods and 8 cloves. Bring to the boil and simmer for 15 minutes. Strain into a jug, cover and refrigerate. This quantity will keep for 4 days; larger amounts will have to be processed and waxed.

Rosehip syrup

Bring 35fl.oz (1lt) of water to the boil. Liquidize 4lb (1.8kg) of rosehips and pour into the water. Simmer for 30 minutes. Remove from heat, and leave for 15 minutes. Return to the heat, add another 35fl.oz (1lt) of water and simmer for 20 minutes. Pour the pulp into a basin, cover and leave overnight.

Place the pulp in a pan and add 2½pts (1.5lt) of water. Boil, then simmer for 20 minutes. Pour into a flannelette square and leave to drip overnight.

Pour the juice into a heavy pan and put on a low heat. Add 2lb (895g) of sugar and stir until it dissolves. Boil for 5 minutes. Strain, then bottle, process and wax. The syrup can be poured over puddings or diluted to make a rich vitamin C drink.

Elderberry syrup

The fruits of the elder tree ripen between August and October. They are ready for picking when the clusters of reddish-black berries hang towards the ground. Their medicinal properties have been promoted since Druidic times.

Take 4lb (1.8kg) of stalked and washed elderberries. Place them in a heavy pan on a very low heat for 30 minutes, mashing occasionally. Pour the purée into a muslin square and drain overnight.

Pour the juice into a pan, add 1¼lb (560g) of granulated sugar, and six cloves. Bring to the boil and cook for 5 minutes. Re-strain to remove the scum. Pour into a jug, then into bottles. Process and wax.

Dilute to taste and serve as a refreshing iced drink, or as a hot tonic for colds and influenza.

Cucumber & iced mint tea

You can use a combination of mints, peppermint, French apple, Eau de Cologne, etc. Freeze some of the leaves in ice cubes before making the drink — see page 80.

Gather the leaves and wash them thoroughly under cold running water. Shake them dry in a colander. Weigh 6oz (170g) of mint, place in a pan and cover with 35fl.oz (1lt) of cold water. Slice half a cucumber thinly, and add to the mint. Bring to the boil and simmer for 15 minutes. Strain the liquid into a jug, cover, and refrigerate.

Serve in glasses with the minted ice cubes, a sprig of fresh mint and two slices of cucumber.

This quantity will keep for no longer than 4 days in the refrigerator. Larger amounts must be processed.

Hazel-honey drink

The small hazel tree can be found in most wood and wasteland areas and it grows abundantly in hedgerows. Gather the nuts from September onwards and look carefully, as it is sometimes difficult to distinguish them from the yellow autumn leaves. The nuts are formed in sets of two or three and each is half covered by small soft leaves. They may be creamy in colour but will soon turn brown.

If the nuts are out of season, you can buy them at groceries or health-food stores.

Chop 8oz (225g) of hazelnuts and put them through a coffee grinder, or liquidize them. Add 1¼pt (¾lt) of milk and 6 tblsp of honey. Whisk. Serve chilled. You will have a delicious protein-packed drink.

Pear and yoghurt tea

This unusual combination of tea, yoghurt and honey makes a refreshing and nourishing drink.

Put 4 tablespoons of un-scented tea in a basin and cover with 35fl.oz (1lt) of cold water. Leave the tea to steep overnight.

Strain the tea liquor. Take 4 medium-sized pears and peel them as finely as possible. Cut each into four, removing all the core, place in a large bowl and mash with a fork. Add 10fl.oz (285ml) of plain yoghurt and 2 tablespoons of clear honey. Pour in the tea liquor and whisk thoroughly. Serve chilled.

It is advisable to drink this tea within 2 days of making, especially in warm weather, as the yoghurt may begin to ferment.

Scents and fragrances

Introduction

I am sure you are often enchanted and refreshed by the fragrances of flowers and fruits when you are walking in gardens, fields or woodlands, and wish you could, so to speak, pluck them out of the air and take them home with you!

Our ancestors used to fill their homes with these natural scents and this chapter recalls many of the ways in which they did this. I always remember the fragrance of oranges and lavender which used to fill my grandparents' house. My grandmother loved lavender and used to make dozens of small lavender pouches which she patiently embroidered and then hid among her clothes and linen in drawers, cupboards and chests. When she came to stay at Christmas, she brought with her the same lavender-orange smell which lingered in the house for days after she had left.

Centuries before cans of 'fresh air' and toilet deodorizers were available people would scent their homes with natural fragrances. Sweet-smelling grasses were strewn on cottage floors. Herbs and flowers were gathered and dried to make sweet bags and herb pillows. Larger Elizabethan homes had their own still-rooms where the mistress of the house made herbal waters, pot-pourris, scented beads, pomanders and any number of delightful concoctions. The Bible mentions many aromatic perfumes; frankincense, calamus root, myrrh and cassia bark. The Egyptians, Greeks and Romans made use in their homes of exotic fragrances derived from roots, bark, leaves and petals.

Today we can experience the same beautiful aromas which were commonplace in the ancient and medieval worlds and this chapter aims to help you to do just that — to fill your homes with naturally subtle scents and fragrances.

All the ingredients mentioned can be bought from herbalists, chemists, or specialists (in England, mostly London based) but many can be home-grown, picked and dried with greater satisfaction and less expense. If you experience any difficulty in obtaining the ingredients please write to the publishers for advice.

Special equipment is not required but a hand or electric coffee grinder is necessary for roots, bark and citrus peel. A mortar and pestle are useful too, but an ordinary basin and the back of a tablespoon make excellent substitutes.

Essential equipment

Small coffee grinder for grinding spices etc; various basins and bowls; tablespoon; teaspoon; knife; saucepan; screw-topped jars for storing dried herbs; corked or stoppered bottles for fragrant liquids; trimmings – ribbons, lace, miniature flowers, beads etc.

Citrus pomanders

2 thin-skinned citrus fruits
  (oranges, lemons or limes)
3oz (85g) whole cloves
1 tblsp orris root powder
1 tblsp ground cinnamon
wooden cocktail sticks
various trimmings for decoration

The original pomander — 'apple of amber' — of the
Tudor and Stuart period, was made from hardened
fixatives such as ambergris, musk and civet. This
sweet-smelling ball, about the size of a crab apple, was

Citrus pomanders make beautiful Christmas gifts

enclosed in an ornate case of ivory, crystal, gold or
silver and hung from bracelets, necklaces and belts.
There were several reasons for wearing a pomander.
Plague was rampant in those times and the scent of
perfumed articles worn about the person was believed
to purify the pestilential air. People seldom or never
bathed so the aromatic perfume of the pomander
helped to cover up stale body odour.

The pomanders bought in shops today are usually
a collection of fragrant herbs and petals with fixative
and a few drops of essential oil added. These are

97

encased in a delicately painted china ball which has holes at the top to emit the perfume.

There are two types of citrus pomander. One version has the flesh completely removed from a hole in the top of the fruit. The shell of peel is left to dry and then filled with crushed spice and fixatives. The second, illustrated on page 97, is pierced with whole cloves and carefully rolled in a mixture of fixatives and finely ground herbs or spices. It is left to dry out for 3–4 weeks and can then be decorated.

If you wish to tie a ribbon round the pomander, leave a wide channel (remember that the fruit will shrink) when pressing in the cloves. You can work directly into the fruit, but if the skin is rather thick the clove tops may break. If this happens, make the holes with cocktail sticks first.

Mix the orris root powder and ground cinnamon in a small bowl, pressing out any lumps with the back of a spoon. Take the fruit, which is now covered with cloves (apart from the areas to be decorated) and roll it in the spice mixture. Wrap the pomander in tissue paper and leave it among your clothes in a closed cupboard or drawer for 3–4 weeks.

The pomander will now be partially dried out. Blow off any excess powder and then decorae it with lace, ribbons, dried flowers or any pretty knick-knack. It will, over a long period, shrink still further and become rock-hard but the perfume will last for years and give your clothes or linen a special fragrance.

Perfumed beads

Perfumed beads are a smaller version of the original pomander. As the name suggests, fixatives, spices and other fragrant powders are combined with liquid gum, formed into bead shapes, strung and then left to harden. The perfume from these small beads can last for many years: I have some hanging in my wardrobe which are over five years old and they still emit a lovely perfume which is as potent as it was when I first made them. Some beads have been known to retain their scent for more than twenty-five years.

Grind all the dry ingredients and measure them into a basin. Mix well, pressing out small lumps with the back of a spoon. Add the mucilage of tragacanth (see the instructions for making this in the recipe for Incense cones on page 106) and mix to a pliable paste. Add the oil, or oils, and combine the mixture again very thoroughly.

To make equal-sized beads, scoop up a portion of the paste using a very small measuring spoon, then scrape away any excess with a knife. Put the rough portions on a sheet of waxed paper and continue until all the paste has been used. Rub your hands with one of the oils used in the recipe and make balls, cubes or similar shapes with each portion. Place the beads carefully between waxed paper, and leave them to dry out for about two hours.

Lubricate a needle and a length of extra-strong thread with oil. Thread the beads (small round or square glass beads can also be added) and tie knots at both ends, then wrap them carefully in tissue paper. Place them in a dark, dry place for 1 week — a clothes or linen drawer would be suitable — after which they will have shrunk a little and be ready for fastening permanently.

The beads can be made into belts, using a double row and attaching a small buckle; they can be used as necklaces, bracelets, or as a trimming for lampshades.

Lavender beads

2 tblsp ground lavender flowers
1 tblsp ground rosemary needles
1 tblsp orris root powder
1 tblsp ground calamus root
1 tblsp sandalwood powder
2 tblsp mucilage of gum tragacanth
½ teasp lavender oil

Orange beads

2 level tblsp ground orange peel
1 tblsp ground lemon geranium leaves
1 teasp ground dried lemon peel
1 tblsp orris root powder
1 tblsp ground calamus root
2½ tblsp mucilage of gum tragacanth
½ teasp jaffa orange oil

Spice beads

2 tblsp ground cassia bark
1 tblsp ground cloves
1 tblsp powdered gum benzoin
1 teasp ground cinnamon
1 teasp grated nutmeg
1 teasp ground allspice
1 teasp ground cardamom seeds
2 tblsp mucilage of gum tragacanth
3 drops civet oil
½ teasp cedarwood oil

Rose beads

2 tblsp ground rose petals
1 tblsp ground rose geranium leaves
1 teasp sandalwood powder
1 tblsp orris root powder
1 tblsp powdered gum benzoin
2 tblsp mucilage of gum tragacanth
1 teasp rose oil

Perfumed beads, a smaller version of the 'original' pomander, are a mixture of fragrant powders, fixatives and liquid gum. Their scent can last for many years

Sweet-scented bags

These little bags are simple to make. You need pieces of closely woven fabric, cotton, lawn etc.; trimmings; rubber bands and the listed ingredients. The finished bags measure about 3in. × 4in. (7½cm × 10cm).

Cut two pieces of fabric 4in. × 5in. (10cm × 12½cm). With right sides facing, sew three seams, leaving one of the narrow ends open. Neaten the open edge. Turn inside out, press and attach the trimmings.

When decorating your bags you could indicate their fragrance in some way. Little lace roses are made by winding a length of lace trimming tightly, like a catherine wheel, securing it with a few stitches, then sewing a pearl droplet in the centre.

Place the ingredients in a bowl, mix thoroughly and divide equally between two bags. Close the bag with a rubber band and tie with a bowed ribbon or pretty cord.

Sweet-scented bags trimmed with lace, beads and ribbons

Lavender bags

4 tblsp dried lavender flowers; ½ teasp orris root powder; 3 drops lavender oil.

Rose bags

4 tblsp dried rose petals; ½ teasp orris root powder; 8 drops rose oil.

Citrus bags

3 tblsp dried, roughly ground orange and lemon peel; 1 tblsp lemon verbena; 2 drops jaffa orange oil; 2 drops lime oil; 1 drop grass oil.

Fragrant sachets

The little sachets above are filled with fragrant ingredients which are all ground to a rough powder. Unlike the sweet-scented bags they will lie flat and can be tacked to the lining of coats, jackets or hats. They can also be placed inside a writing box to give the paper and envelopes a delicate perfume.

Any finely woven material can be used; calico, silk, lawn or cotton. The sachet, usually about 4in. (10cm) square, can be decorated with ribbons and lace, embroidered or, if it is to be hidden inside a garment, left plain. Square or oblong sachets are simple to make but round or heart-shaped ones can look very pretty.

Slip a fragrant sachet in with your writing notelets

The ingredients (given overleaf) for the two recipes can be bought from herbalists, but you may be able to pick and dry some of them yourself.

The elder tree grows in hedgerows, on waste land and in woods. Clusters of its little cream flowers can be gathered from the beginning of May to the end of June.

Potted rose geraniums are available at many garden centres and cuttings can easily be taken; detach a stem, including the heel, and remove the lower leaves. Put the stem into a small pot of moist compost and cover

101

Pull them gently from the flower-head and dry them in a warm airy room on a piece of absorbent fabric stretched between the backs of two chairs. Herbs should be picked just before the plants bloom, and dried in the same way.

Spices always have a more poignant aroma if they are ground just before you use them.

Other dried flowers, nasturtiums, borage, corn-flowers and marigold petals may also be included to add extra splashes of bright colour.

4 cups dried rose petals
2 cups dried rose geranium leaves
1 cup dried lavender flowers
1 cup dried elderflowers
2 tblsp dried ground orange peel
1 tblsp dried ground lemon peel
2 teasp freshly ground cloves

2 teasp freshly ground allspice
2 teasp freshly ground cardamom seeds
1 tblsp everlasting flowers
2 tblsp orris root powder
1 teasp rose oil
½ teasp sandalwood oil
3 drops lavender oil

The above ingredients will make the pot-pourri shown on the previous page. Mix them all in a large basin, but adding the orris root powder and oils last. Mix again, thoroughly but gently, then cover the basin and leave to mature in a dry dark place for 3 weeks. Give the mixture a gentle stir every 3–4 days.

Transfer the pot-pourris to pretty lidded bowls or dishes. Remove the lids when you want to fill your rooms with subtle fragrances. The scent will be more noticeable when the room is warm.

Scented candles

Candle-making has a long and interesting history. The Greeks and Romans made candles by dipping threads of flax into a mixture of pitch and beeswax. Constantine the Great built the first European Christian church and ordered scented candles always to be burned there.

During the middle ages country folk made their candles from rendered animal fats. Wealthier people could afford to buy beeswax candles which had a smooth finish and gave a longer, brighter light.

Early settlers in America used to collect wax from the berries of the bayberry tree. The berries were gathered in the fall, or autumn, and poured into large tubs of boiling water. When the wax floated to the top it was scooped out and pressed into small cakes. A cotton wick was inserted during the shaping. When the candles were burned they gave off a delicate perfume.

Candle-making equipment
Various moulds

1lb (445g) block of paraffin wax (or granules)
3 teasp stearic acid
different coloured wax crayons or wax dye
candle perfume or essential oils
a card of thick wick
a little cooking oil
adhesive tape and modelling clay, or mould seal

For moulds you can use any small cylindrical or square containers which will tolerate high temperatures. Food cans make excellent moulds. Make sure that the tops are smooth, cut away the rim with scissors. Experience will tell you how much wax to use for the size of mould. It is better to have too much wax than too little. Any excess can be re-melted and used again.

Cover your working surface with newspaper. Put the wax into a basin over a pan of boiling water. While it is melting, lightly brush the inside of your mould with cooking oil. Pierce a small hole in the bottom of the mould with a sharp pointed knife. Thread a length of wick through the hole, leaving 1in. (2.5cm) protruding from the hole and 1in. (2.5cm) above the top of the mould. Put the open end of the mould on your working surface and stick adhesive tape over the hole and the protruding wick to ensure that the melted wax will not leak out. As an extra precaution, cover the whole base with a piece of flattened clay. To make sure that the wick is centred at the top, wrap the extra 1in. (2.5cm) of wick around a pencil, securing it with adhesive tape. Lay the pencil across the mould and tape it in position.

When the wax has melted, add the recommended amount of stearic acid. When this has dissolved, chop a wax crayon into small pieces and drop them into the wax, or add a special wax dye. Stir until the crayon pieces have melted. Remove the basin from the boiling water and add 1 teaspoon (or more, depending on the size of the mould) of essential oil or candle perfume. Stir, then carefully pour the hot wax into the mould. The base should not leak but if it does, scoop up the wax and put it back into the mould. The leak will stop as soon as the wax begins to cool.

The candle should be set in 2–3 hours. Carefully remove the clay, tape and pencil. Pull the sides of the mould away from the candle then give a sharp bang underneath. If you find that the candle is a little stubborn, you can encourage it by very gently pulling the wick.

Incense cones

Incense is a combination of powdered charcoal and aromatic resins, gums, barks and seeds. It has been used for centuries in religious ceremonies and rituals.

The ingredients below will give off pleasant aromatic fumes. The first mixture is quite sweet, the second is rather like that which is burned in churches.

6 tblsp instant burning charcoal
1 tblsp powdered gum benzoin
1 tblsp each of ground calamus root, ground sandalwood chips and ground cassia bark
1 tblsp dried ground orange peel

Incense cones, historically used in religious rituals

½ teasp musk oil
½ teasp sandalwood oil
3 tblsp mucilage of gum tragacanth

6 tblsp instant burning charcoal
1 tblsp each of powdered gum benzoin, orris root powder and ground cassia bark
1 teasp each of ground cloves, ground cardamom seeds and dried ground lemon peel
1 teasp each of myrrh and frankincense powder
½ teasp frangipani oil
3 tblsp mucilage of gum tragacanth

Gum tragacanth is used as a binder. It can be bought from herbalists in powdered form. To make a mucilage (thick sticky liquid) add 15fl.oz (425ml) of cold water, a little at a time, to ½oz (14g) of tragacanth powder. Press out any lumps with the back of a spoon. Add half a teaspoon of benzoin powder, or tincture of benzoin, to preserve the liquid. Leave the mucilage in a screw-topped jar for 3 days and shake it vigorously twice each day. A quicker and easier way of making the mucilage is to liquidize the water, powder and benzoin (in an electric blender). It can then be put to use on the following day.

Break up the charcoal and measure it into a basin. Add the dry ingredients (if possible buy the spices whole and grind them yourself). Mix well, stir in the mucilage, then add the oils. Combine thoroughly Shape the paste into small cones and place on waxed paper. Transfer to the airing cupboard. The cones will take about a week to dry out completely. Wrap them in tissue paper and store in a box until required.

Please remember that a smouldering cone can be dangerous. Never put uncontained cones in a direct draught, because they are very light and can quite easily be blown onto highly flammable furnishings.

Scented washballs

Scented washballs were popular in the seventeenth and eighteenth centuries. English nobility used the expensive washballs imported from northern Italy where small family industries were involved in their production. The less wealthy made their own scented washballs by grinding home-made soap, adding certain herbs and flowers, then mixing everything to a paste with rose water.

Grate the soap into a basin. Grind the dry ingredients thoroughly, then sieve them over the soap. Mix well.

Slowly add the orange flower or rose water and mix to a pliable paste. Add the oils and combine the mixture thoroughly again. Rub a little essential oil into your palms, take pieces of the mixture, each weighing about 1oz (28g) and roll them into smooth balls. You should be able to make eleven or twelve balls with each of the recipes given below. Put the washballs between pieces of waxed paper and place in an airing cupboard. Leave them to dry for 3–4 days.

Scented washballs, popular with eighteenth-century nobility. The less wealthy used similar recipes to that above

Orange and elderflower washballs

8oz (225g) bar of simple unscented soap
1 heaped tblsp orris root powder
1 heaped teasp sandalwood powder
1 teasp laundry starch (dry)
1 tblsp finely ground elderflowers
8 tblsp orange flower water
½ teasp orange flower oil

Lavender and camomile washballs

8oz (225g) bar of simple unscented soap
1 heaped tblsp ground calamus root
1 teasp orris root powder
1 teasp laundry starch (dry)
2 teap finely ground lavender flowers
2 teasp finely ground camomile
8 tblsp rose water
3 drops each of lavender and sandalwood oil

These washballs make lovely gifts and can be decorated with ribbon, beads or dried flowers which are attached by using bobble headed pins of various colours.

Exotic cream perfume with rose and citrus cologne

Exotic cream perfume

This is a delicate, non-greasy perfume which can be gently applied to all the pulse points.

1 tblsp emulsifying wax
1 tblsp almond oil
½ teasp lanolin
1 level teasp kaolin
½ teasp glycerine
3 tblsp orange flower water
½ teasp ylang ylang oil

Place the wax, almond oil and lanolin in a basin, over a pan of simmering water. When they have melted, gently heat the glycerine, orange flower water and kaolin in a separate basin over another pan of simmering water. Remove both basins from heat and slowly add the orange flower water mixture to the melted oils. Stir continuously until the mixture thickens and begins to cool. Add the frangipani and ylang ylang oils and stir for a few more minutes. While the cream is still cooling, cut a circle of kitchen foil, slightly larger than the top of a pretty screw-topped jar. Transfer the cream perfume to the jar, place the circle of foil neatly over the cream and secure the top.

Rose and citrus cologne

This cologne can be splashed over the body after a shower or bath. The vodka is used as a preservative and also acts as a gentle astringent, stimulating and refreshing to the skin.

6 tblsp fresh fragrant rose petals
10 tblsp vodka
dried peel of 2 oranges
dried peel of 2 lemons
3 teasp fresh sage
1 tblsp dried mint
a cup of boiling water

Pour the vodka into a screw-topped jar. Add the rose petals and leave them to steep for 1 week. Give the jar a vigorous shake twice each day.

On the 6th day put the peel (this can be roughly ground in a coffee grinder or broken into very small pieces), the sage, and mint into a basin. Pour the cup of boiling water over the ingredients, cover with a porous cloth and leave to steep overnight.

Strain the two liquids into a jug using a piece of muslin or doubled cheesecloth. Re-strain until they are perfectly clear. Pour the cologne into a pretty corked or stoppered bottle and use once a week.

Cosmetics

Introduction

This chapter is not a beauty guide, but it is based on the principle that we feel healthier, and consequently happier, when we care for ourselves. Personal hygiene and cleanliness, a balanced diet and regular exercise all contribute to our sense of well-being. This can be extended to include the finer points of care, one of which is skin care.

The skin has many functions. It is waterproof and acts as a protective barrier against bacteria; it helps dispose of toxins and waste matter and also regulates the body temperature. The outer skin (the epidermis) is made up of cells that are divided into two layers. The top layer is composed of dead cells while those underneath are alive. Below these is the true skin (the dermis) which is a soft and fibrous substance. Finally there is a layer of fat.

Skin must be kept clean to enable it to function properly, but continual washing removes the valuable moisture, oils and protective acid mantle. The only alternative to washing with soap and water is either to find another method of cleansing, or to replace the natural substances lost by washing. The cosmetics recipes in this chapter are designed to fulfil both of these needs, and they include as many natural ingredients as possible. They are quite simple to make and you will already have some of the ingredients in your kitchen — honey, cucumber, cider vinegar and soap flakes. The others can be bought from most herbalists, but if you do have difficulty in obtaining any of them please write to the publishers for advice.

You will discover that some of the recipes, for example Elderflower cleansing milk on page 114, look rather different in colour from that which the name suggests. This is because only pure, natural ingredients are used. Any home-made cosmetic based on a herbal infusion will be darker than any of its commercial counterparts. You will also notice that many recipes include an optional essential oil. If you have a particularly sensitive skin, it is safer to omit this.

If you suffer from any serious skin disorders, it may be wiser to consult your doctor before using any of the preparations.

Producing your first jar of home-made cream will give you a feeling of satisfaction and pride, and probably mild surprise — it really is so easy!

Essential equipment

Saucepans to use as 'double pans' when melting and blending the waxes; various heat-resistant bowls and basins to use in conjunction with the pans; egg whisk or fork; tablespoon and teaspoons; muslin or similar fabric for straining herbs and flowers; kitchen foil to cover creams before securing the lids; various corked or stoppered bottles for the cosmetic lotions and screw-topped jars for the different creams.

Herbal face steamer

1 tblsp dried camomile
1 tblsp dried rosemary needles
1 tblsp dried comfrey
about 20 fresh nettle leaves
¾ teasp gum arabic
1 tblsp cider vinegar
several slices of cucumber

Steaming is probably the very best method of insuring that the face is perfectly clean. The herbs used in this recipe have properties which will help to cleanse, heal and stimulate the skin.

The stimulating cleanser — Herbal face steamer

Place the dried herbs, nettle leaves and gum arabic in a medium-sized basin and slowly add 17½ fl.oz (½lt) of boiling water. Leaning over the basin, cover your head and the whole basin with a heavy towel. Steam your face for about 15 minutes.

Now that the pores are open, any stubborn blackheads can be gently removed. Dab these areas with cider vinegar, then close the pores by patting the entire face with slices of cucumber. (You will smell rather like a salad dressing for about 10 minutes!)

Note: If you have a serious skin disorder or badly broken veins it is best *not* to use the steam method.

Cleansing cream

4 teasp white beeswax
2 tblsp anhydrous lanolin
4 tblsp almond oil
2 tblsp baby oil
2 tblsp rose water
¼ teasp borax
3 drops essential rose oil (optional)

A cream very similar to this recipe was developed nearly two thousand years ago by the Greeks.

Melt the beeswax and lanolin separately, then measure them into a basin over a pan of simmering water and blend in the almond and baby oils. Remove from heat. Dissolve the borax in the rose water. Stir the waxes and oils continuously, and slowly add the rose water, stirring until the mixture cools and begins to thicken.

(To quicken the process, put the basin in a pan of cold water, but keep stirring.) Blend in the rose oil (optional). Put the cream in a screw-topped jar, cover with a circle of kitchen foil and secure the lid.

Apply gently to the face and throat. Leave for a few minutes, then remove with cotton wool soaked in an equal mixture of witch hazel and rose water. If you have very dry skin use 3 parts of rose water to 1 part of witch hazel.

Creams for cleansing (the white one) and nourishing

Apple blossom body lotion

8fl.oz (225ml) water
5 tblsp soap flakes (not detergent)
9 teasp almond oil
6 teasp olive oil
1½ teasp glycerine
1½ teasp vodka (or witch hazel)
3 drops essential apple blossom oil
2 drops red food colouring

This is a lovely silky lotion which should be applied to the body after a shower or bath. Soap flakes are a form of very mild, pure soap which, when combined with the oils, will not dry the skin.

Put the water into a pan, and place it on a low heat. Add the soap flakes and stir until they dissolve. Remove from heat and stir in the two oils, glycerine and vodka (or witch hazel). Stir until the mixture cools. Blend in the essential oil and food colouring. Pour into a stoppered bottle and keep in the bathroom.

If the lotion becomes very cold it may solidify. Should this happen, place the bottle in a basin of warm water, over a pan of boiling water. Pour the heated lotion (which will solidify again as it begins to cool) into a pretty screw-topped jar. It can be used just as effectively as a cream.

Apply silky Apple blossom body lotion after a bath

Oatmeal face scrub

3 teasp medium ground oatmeal
2 teasp ground almonds
2 teasp fuller's earth
2 teasp dried ground orange peel
juice of 1 lemon
1 tblsp clear honey
1 soft apple mashed to a pulp

A facial scrub is used as a gentle abrasive. It will remove dead skin and unblock the pores.

Orange peel granules can be bought from most herbalists, but it is cheaper to make your own. Save all orange peel, remove as much pith as possible and dry it in an airing cupboard or on a sunny window-sill. When the peel is dry and brittle, break it into small pieces and grind to a rough powder in a coffee grinder.

Place all the dry ingredients in a basin and bind them together with the lemon juice, honey and apple pulp. Apply to the face with gentle circular movements. Relax the facial muscles and leave the scrub on for 10 minutes. Rinse off with tepid water, pat the face dry, then use a skin tonic or a little rose water.

This recipe will give 5 or 6 applications. Put the remaining mixture into a screw-topped jar and store in the refrigerator until required.

Egg-white face mask

1 small egg white
2 teasp fuller's earth
1 teasp almond oil
1 teasp wheatgerm oil
3 drops tincture of myrrh

This mask has a gentle astringent action which combines with the softening properties of the wheatgerm and almond oils. It will leave your face feeling both soft and stimulated.

Separate the egg, letting the white fall into a basin (the yolk could be added to Protein hair care or Bergamot sun tan oil, opposite). Beat the egg white with a fork or egg whisk until it becomes stiff. Fold in the fuller's earth, then stir in the wheatgerm and almond oils and the tincture of myrrh.

Spread a thin film of the mixture over the face and throat. Relax the facial muscles and leave the mask on for 15–20 minutes. Rinse off with cool water. Pat dry, then, using cotton wool, apply a mixture of 1 part witch hazel to 3 parts rose water (or equal parts of each for very greasy skin).

There should be enough mixture for at least 2 applications. You could share it with a friend when it is freshly made, or transfer it to a screw-topped jar and store in the refrigerator for a few days.

Protein hair care

1 large egg
1 tblsp wheatgerm oil
2 teasp glycerine
1 teasp cider vinegar
To make the infusion:
3 tblsp dried rosemary needles *or*
    3 tblsp dried camomile
3 cups boiling water

This is suitable for all types of hair. It should be rubbed well into the scalp after the hair has been washed with a good brand of ordinary or herbal shampoo.

Blend the 4 ingredients together in a basin. Pour the mixture into a screw-topped bottle and store in the refrigerator until required. The above recipe should be enough for 2–3 applications.

Leave the mixture on the scalp for about 15 minutes. Rinse off with an infusion of rosemary for dark hair, or camomile for fair hair.

The infusion should be made 1 hour before washing the hair. Put the herbs into a basin, pour the boiling water over them, cover with a porous cloth and leave for 1 hour. Strain through doubled muslin (or a similar material) into a jug and cover until required. The rinse should be poured over the hair several times in order to gain full benefit from the herbal properties.

114

Bergamot sun tan oil

3 tblsp olive oil
2 tblsp sesame oil
1 tblsp wheatgerm oil
6 drops essential bergamot oil
3 drops essential lavender oil
1 tblsp cider vinegar
1 large egg yolk

Bergamot oil is used as a base for many of the sun tan preparations, particularly in the south of France. Apart from having a lovely perfume, it seems to speed up the tanning process. Also the oil of lavender helps

Protection from sun and water for body and hands

to discourage flies and other insects.

Use an egg whisk to blend the five oils in a basin. Continue beating gently and add the vinegar. Finally, add the egg yolk (the white could be used for the Egg face mask, opposite). Beat until the ingredients are thoroughly combined. Pour into an opaque glass (or plastic) bottle and store in the fridge until required.

Shake the bottle vigorously before using the oil, and apply it generously to all exposed parts. (If you have been in the sun without the protection of an oil, a solution of strong tea will relieve any burning. Cucumber and raw potato are also soothing.)

Soaps

Please read this introduction before making any soap

The origin of soap is a mystery but one engaging suggestion is that some Roman women discovered it by accident about 3000 years ago. They washed their clothes where rain water fell from the hills into the river Tiber and over altars on which animals had been slaughtered. The fat from the sacrifice and ashes from the fire are said to have combined as the first crude soap.

Making soap at home is an interesting and satisfying activity. It is very simple, for you need no special equipment beyond a few basic ingredients and some pliable plastic moulds.

The main ingredients are *water, caustic soda* and *tallow*. You can add other substances to give the soap more lather or a delicate colour and perfume, or to make it softer or more abrasive. *Caustic soda* is obtainable from hardware stores and chemists. *Tallow* is made by rendering (melting down) lumps of animal fat which you can beg or buy from your butcher; 2lb or 1kg should be enough to start with. Render it in a heavy pan over a low heat and strain it into warm, screw-topped jars. The tallow should be free from impurities, streaks of blood, bits of meat, etc. If you can, keep it in a refrigerator until required.

Please remember that *caustic soda is very dangerous* if used without care. Wear rubber gloves and a strong plastic apron (covering as much of you as possible) throughout the soap-making process. Never try to make soap when children are about; they are far too curious and their first instinct is to touch. Any contact with caustic soda, or even newly made soaps, will burn and burn painfully. I make my soaps when the children are at school or safely in bed.

Once you have made basic white soap you will want to try the more adventurous recipes. You must have all the ingredients to hand, and at the right temperature, before you start.

You can buy most of the oils — sunflower, safflower, olive, etc. — from health food stores and chemists. Some firms supply essential oils (extracted from flowers, herbs leaves and spices) by mail order. Send for their catalogues and compare prices.

For convenience, all the measures in this chapter are given in teaspoons (teasp), tablespoons (tblsp) or cups — use an ordinary tea cup holding about 9fl.oz.

Remember

Caustic soda can damage people and things. If it touches your skin, use the ancient remedy of rinsing with water and applying fresh lemon juice or vinegar. If the effect seems at all severe, consult a doctor at once. Some people are allergic to certain ingredients, so read the recipes carefully to make sure they contain none of your known allergens. If you have sensitive skin, proceed with caution.

Basic equipment

Strong plastic apron; a pair of rubber gloves; sheets of newspaper for covering work surface; saucepan; heat-resistant basin; heat-resistant jug; average-sized tea cup holding approx. 9fl.oz; tablespoon; teaspoon; wooden spoon; egg whisk; various pliable plastic moulds — margarine tubs, dessert containers etc.

Basic white soap

The white soap recipe is used as a basis for all the soaps in this chapter. You will need:

1 cup cold water
2 tblsp caustic soda
one cup melted tallow

Protect your working surface with several sheets of newspaper. Wear rubber gloves and an apron, and pour the cold water into a heat-resistant bowl. Add the caustic soda and stir it immediately with a wooden spoon. Do not stand directly over the bowl as the fumes can be dangerous. The tallow and the soda should be lukewarm when mixed together; put your hands under the bowl to see if the caustic solution is cool enough. Slowly pour the lukewarm tallow into the solution, stirring continuously. Beat gently with an

Basic white soap, very simple to make. All the soaps on the following pages are variations of this recipe

egg whisk for 4 minutes. Pour the mixture into 2–3 clean margarine tubs (or any pliable plastic moulds, see under Basic equipment) and leave to set on one side for 6 hours — well away from children.

Carefully ease the soaps out of their moulds and transfer onto a piece of kitchen roll. Allow them to mature in a dry, airy place (out of children's way) for at least 2 weeks.

When your soap is a few days old you will notice a fine white powder on the surface. This is sodium carbonate and results from the exposure of caustic soda to the air. Wash it away when the soap is mature as it tends to make the skin dry.

Children's strawberry soap

Spiced egg soap

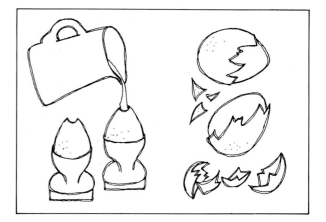

Children's strawberry soap

½ cup cold water
2 tblsp caustic soda
¼ cup melted tallow
¼ cup baby oil
¼ cup olive oil
2 teasp essential strawberry oil
¼ cup rape oil
1 tblsp melted lanolin
1 tblsp melted coconut oil
2 teasp red food colour
3 rubber moulds, stiff card, and 3 tumblers

Take 3 pieces of stiff card and cut a hole in each, large enough to support the base of the mould. Place the card supporting the mould in a tumbler or similar container (the mould should not touch the sides or bottom of the tumbler).

Protect the working surface with several sheets of newspaper. Wearing your rubber gloves and apron, pour the cold water into a heat-resistant bowl. Add the caustic soda and stir immediately with a wooden spoon. Test to see whether the solution is lukewarm (see Basic white soap on page 117), then slowly add the lukewarm tallow, stirring continuously. Beat with an egg whisk for 1 minute. Continue beating gently

Strawberry-perfumed soap for children's bath time

and add the baby oil, olive oil, rape oil, strawberry oil, food colour, melted lanolin and melted coconut oil. Beat for a few seconds, then pour the mixture quickly into the moulds (these can be bought from most art and craft shops). Leave to set for 36 hours.

Rub a thin film of washing-up liquid over each of the moulds and carefully peel them back. Put the soaps onto a piece of kitchen roll and leave them to mature in a dry, airy place for 3 weeks — well away from children's reach for the time being!

Spiced egg soap

½ cup cold water
2 tblsp caustic soda
½ cup melted tallow
1 teasp essential clove oil
1 teasp essential cinnamon oil
½ cup rape oil
1 teasp cold water
1 teasp turmeric
3 medium-sized eggs

To blow the eggs for use as moulds pierce a hole with a darning needle at each end of one of the eggs. Hold the

119

egg over a basin and blow out the contents. Now make a hole at the broad end of the egg, large enough to take liquid poured from a jug. Do the same with the remaining eggs then wash them all thoroughly. Shake dry and place in a cool oven for 30 minutes. Seal the smaller hole of each egg with strips of self-adhesive tape. Put the eggs in egg cups. Mix the turmeric with the teaspoonful of cold water.

Protect the working surface with several sheets of newspaper. Wearing rubber gloves and an apron, pour the cold water into a heat-resistant bowl. Add the caustic soda and stir immediately with a wooden spoon. Test to see if the solution is lukewarm (see Basic white soap on page 117) then slowly add the

lukewarm tallow, stirring continuously. Beat with an egg whisk for 1 minute. Continue beating gently and add the two essential oils, rape oil and turmeric water. Beat for 1 more minute, then transfer the mixture to a jug. Pour slowly into the shells. The mixture will reduce as it dries, so keep topping it up for the next 10 minutes. Leave to set for 36 hours.

Peel away the egg shells very carefully. Put the soaps on a piece of kitchen roll and allow to mature in a dry, airy place for at least 2 weeks — well out of children's reach.

Spiced egg soap. Turmeric causes the speckled effect

Green herbal soap

½ cup of cold water and a bunch of fresh thyme
2 tblsp caustic soda
¼ cup caster oil
½ cup melted lard
¼ cup rape oil
1 tblsp melted coconut oil
3 drops of rosemary, sage, bergamot and spearmint oil

Cut the bunch of fresh thyme into small pieces and steep it in the cold water for 3 hours.

Protect the working surface with several sheets of newspaper. Strain the thyme water into a heat-resistant bowl. Wearing rubber gloves and an apron, add the caustic soda and stir immediately with a wooden spoon. Test to see whether the solution is lukewarm, then slowly add the lukewarm lard. Beating gently with an egg whisk, add the caster oil, rape oil, essential oils and melted coconut oil. Beat for a few seconds, then pour the mixture into clean, pliable plastic moulds. Leave to set for 48 hours.

Gently ease the soaps out of their moulds. Transfer them to a piece of kitchen roll, and leave to mature in a dry, airy place for at least 2 weeks — well out of children's reach.

Little mousse tubs were used for this green herbal soap

Yellow rose soap

¼ cup cold water
2 tblsp caustic soda
½ cup melted tallow
½ cup rose water
½ cup almond oil
¼ cup melted coconut oil
2 teasp essential rose oil
1 teasp green food colour

Protect the working surface with several sheets of newspaper. Wearing rubber gloves and an apron, pour the cold water into a heat-resistant bowl. Add the caustic soda and stir immediately with a wooden spoon. Test to see if the solution is lukewarm (see Basic white soap on page 117), then slowly add the lukewarm tallow, stirring continuously. Beat with an egg whisk for 1 minute. Continue beating gently and add the castor oil, olive oil, freesia oil, melted lanolin, rose oil and green colour. Beat for 1 minute more, then pour the mixture into clean moulds (it may be possible to buy a rubber mould, normally used for plaster of Paris, in the form of a rose). Leave to set for 48 hours.

Gently ease the soaps out of their moulds. Transfer them to a piece of kitchen roll and leave to mature in a dry, airy place for at least 2 weeks.

Rich lanolin soap

½ cup cold water
2 tblsp caustic soda
¼ cup melted tallow
2 teasp essential freesia oil
¼ cup olive oil
¼ cup melted coconut oil
¼ cup melted lanolin
¼ cup olive oil

Protect the working surface with several sheets of newspaper. Wearing rubber gloves and an apron, pour the cold water into a heat-resistant bowl. Add the caustic soda and stir immediately with a wooden spoon. Test to see if the solution is lukewarm (see Basic white soap on page 117), then slowly add the lukewarm tallow, stirring continuously. Beat with an egg whisk for 1 minute. Continue beating gently and add the castor oil, olive oil, freesia oil, melted lanolin and melted coconut oil. Pour the mixture into pliable plastic moulds (for these soaps I use little square tubs from frozen trifles). Put the soap to one side and leave it to set for 12 hours.

Gently ease the soaps out of their moulds. Transfer them to a piece of kitchen roll and leave to mature in a dry, airy place for at least 2 weeks.

Cornmeal health soap

¼ cup cold water
2 tblsp caustic soda
½ cup melted tallow
½ cup olive oil
2 teasp essential sandalwood oil
1 teasp wheatgerm oil
¼ cup witch hazel
1 tblsp cornmeal

Protect the working surface with several sheets of newspaper. Add the cornmeal to the witch hazel and stir well. Wearing rubber gloves and an apron, pour the cold water into a heat-resistant bowl. Add the caustic soda and stir immediately with a wooden spoon. Test to see whether the solution is lukewarm (see Basic white soap, page 117), then slowly add the lukewarm tallow, stirring continuously. Beat with an egg whisk for 1 minute. Continue beating gently and add the olive oil, wheatgerm oil, sandalwood oil and witch hazel. Beat for 1 minute more, then pour the mixture into plain (not fluted) pliable plastic moulds. Put on one side and leave to set for 24 hours.

Gently ease the soaps out of their moulds. Transfer them to a piece of kitchen roll, and leave to mature in a dry, airy place for at least 2 weeks.

Sage and cucumber soap

½ cup cold water
bunch fresh sage
2 tblsp caustic soda
½ cup melted lard
1 teasp essential sage oil
¼ cup sunflower oil
¼ cup almond oil
half small cucumber

Cut the bunch of fresh sage into small pieces, and steep it in the cold water for 3 hours. Chop the cucumber (unpeeled) as finely as possible, or liquidize it with a tablespoon of cold water.

Protect the working surface with several sheets of newspaper. Strain the sage water into a heat-resistant bowl. Wearing rubber gloves and an apron, add the caustic soda and stir immediately with a wooden spoon. Test to see if the solution is lukewarm then slowly add the lukewarm lard. Beating gently with an egg whisk, add the 3 oils and 4 level tablespoons of the cucumber pulp. Beat for 1 minute, then pour the mixture into clean, pliable plastic moulds. Put on one side and leave to set for 48 hours.

Gently ease the soaps out of their moulds. Transfer them to a piece of kitchen roll and leave to mature in a dry, airy place for at least 2 weeks.

Camomile milk soap

¼ cup cold water
2 tblsp caustic soda
½ cup melted tallow
¼ cup each almond and safflower oil
2 teasp essential rose geranium oil
1 teasp wheatgerm oil
12 tblsp milk and 2 tblsp dried camomile
plastic ice cube tray

Pour the milk into a small basin and add the dried camomile. Cover with a piece of kitchen roll and leave to steep for 3 hours.

Protect the working surface with several sheets of newspaper. Strain the camomile milk into a cup or jug. Wearing rubber gloves and an apron, pour the cold water into a heat-resistant bowl. Add the caustic soda and stir immediately with a wooden spoon. Test to see if the solution is lukewarm, then slowly add the lukewarm tallow. Beat for 1 minute. Continue beating gently and add the 4 oils and camomile milk. Beat for 1 more minute, then pour the mixture into clean ice cube moulds and leave to set for 24 hours.

Gently ease the soaps out of their moulds. Transfer them to a piece of kitchen roll and leave to mature in a dry, airy place for at least 2 weeks.

Camomile milk soap made in ice cube moulds

Pine solid shampoo

½ cup cold water
2 tblsp caustic soda
½ cup olive oil
¼ cup caster oil
½ cup melted coconut oil
2 teasp essential pine oil

Protect the working surface with several sheets of newspaper. Wearing rubber gloves and an apron, pour the cold water into a heat-resistant bowl. Add the caustic soda and stir immediately with a wooden spoon. Test to see if the solution is lukewarm (see Basic white soap on page 117), then slowly add the lukewarm coconut oil, stirring continuously. Beat gently with an egg whisk and, at the same time, add the olive oil, caster oil and pine oil. Pour the mixture into clean, pliable plastic moulds (do not have the moulds too large: the finished soap should fit comfortably into the palm of the hand). Leave to set for 48 hours.

Gently ease the soaps out of their moulds. Transfer to a piece of kitchen roll. This is a very soft soap, so take care not to squash it! Leave the soap to dry and mature in an airy place — well out of the way of children — for at least 2 weeks.

Cinnamon soap

½ cup cold water
2 tblsp caustic soda
½ cup melted tallow
2 teasp essential cinnamon oil
¼ cup almond oil
¼ cup safflower oil

Protect the working surface with several sheets of newspaper. Wearing rubber gloves and an apron, pour the cold water into a heat-resistant bowl. Add the caustic soda and stir immediately with a wooden spoon. Test to see if the solution is lukewarm (see Basic white soap on page 117), then slowly add the lukewarm tallow, stirring continuously. Beat with an egg whisk for 1 minute. Continue beating gently, then add the almond oil, safflower oil and cinnamon oil. Beat for 1 minute more, then pour the mixture into pliable plastic moulds (for this soap I use oblong margarine tubs). Put on one side and leave to set for 12 hours.

Gently ease the soaps out of their moulds. Transfer them to a piece of kitchen roll and leave to mature in a dry, airy place (well out of children's reach) for at least 2 weeks. This larger, spicy soap makes an ideal gift for a man.

Lavender candle soap

½ cup cold water
2 tblsp caustic soda
¾ cup melted tallow
¼ cup rape oil
1 teasp essential lavender oil
1 teasp red food colour
2 teasp blue food colour
3 rubber candle moulds

Take 3 pieces of stiff card and cut a hole in each, large enough to support the base of the mould. Place the card supporting the mould in a tumbler (the mould should not touch the bottom or sides).

Protect the working surface with several sheets of newspaper. Wearing rubber gloves and an apron, pour the cold water into a heat-resistant bowl. Add the caustic soda and stir immediately with a wooden spoon. Test to see if the solution is lukewarm, then slowly add the lukewarm tallow, stirring continuously. Beat with an egg whisk for 1 minute. Continue beating gently and add the rape oil, lavender oil and food colour. Beat for 1 minute more, then pour the mixture into the rubber moulds. Leave to set for 48 hours.

Rub a thin film of washing-up liquid over each of the moulds and peel them back. Place the soaps carefully onto a piece of kitchen roll and leave them to mature in a dry, airy place for at least 2 weeks.

Carved orange flower bars

2 cups cold water
8 tblsp caustic soda
1½ cups melted tallow
¾ cup olive oil
3 teasp essential orange flower oil
¾ cup melted coconut oil
3 teasp orange food colour
small shoe box and sheet of polythene

Line the shoe box with the polythene, using staples or paper clips to secure it neatly. Place several sheets of newspaper on your working surface. Wearing rubber gloves and an apron, pour the cold water into a heat-resistant bowl. Add the caustic soda and stir immediately with a wooden spoon. Test to see whether the solution is lukewarm, then slowly add the lukewarm tallow, stirring continually. Beat with an egg whisk for 1 minute. Continue beating gently, add the 3 oils and food colour. Beat for 1 minute, then pour into the lined shoe box. Leave to set for 24 hours.

Wearing rubber gloves, carefully remove the slab and place it on a chopping board. With an unserrated sharp knife cut the soap into bars of varying sizes. Put these onto a piece of kitchen roll and leave to mature in a dry, airy place for 3 weeks.

The bars can now be carved into decorative shapes. A lino cutter is useful for surface engraving.

English garden soap

½ cup cold water
2 tblsp caustic soda
½ cup melted tallow
¼ cup olive oil
2 teasp English garden pot-pourri oil
¼ cup melted coconut oil
1½ teasp each of green and yellow food colouring

Protect the working surface with several sheets of newspaper. Wearing rubber gloves and an apron, pour the cold water into a heat-resistant bowl. Add the caustic soda and stir immediately with a wooden spoon. Test to see whether the solution is lukewarm,

English garden soap, perfumed with fragrant pot-pourri

then slowly add the lukewarm tallow, stirring continuously. Beat with an egg whisk for 1 minute. Continue to beat gently and add the olive oil, pot-pourri oil, food colour and melted coconut oil. Beat for 1 minute more, then pour the mixture into clean moulds (those used for the soaps above were from a sheet of plastic compartments for holding yoghurt cartons). Put to one side and leave to set for 36 hours.

Gently ease the soaps out of their moulds and place on a piece of kitchen roll. Leave them to mature in a dry, airy place for at least 2 weeks.

125

GLOSSARY

Allspice: the dried, unripe berry of the pimento or Jamaican pepper tree, native of Central and South America and the West Indies. Has culinary uses.

Almond oil: extracted from the kernel of the almond nut. The almond tree grows in Mediterranean areas and Southern California. The oil has culinary and cosmetic uses.

Ambergris oil: extracted from the intestinal secretions of the sperm whale. Used in perfumes or as a fixative in scents and creams.*

Anhydrous lanolin: the thick sticky fat from sheep's wool. Will absorb twice its weight of water. Widely used in cosmetics.

Annatto: natural vegetable extract used to give an orange colour to cheese or butter.

Aniseed: referred to as either a herb or a spice. The two varieties are green anise which is an annual and grows in Mediterranean areas; and star anise (Chinese anise) found throughout the Orient. Both have culinary and medicinal uses.

Avocado oil: extracted from the fruit, has culinary and cosmetic uses. The avocado tree, a member of the laurel family, is a native of South and Central America.

Bay leaf: aromatic leaf from the evergreen shrub-like tree of Mediterranean areas.

Bergamot oil: extracted from the rind of an orange-like citrus fruit. Used to perfume colognes, also used in sun-tan lotions.

Bicarbonate of soda: a white colourless crystalline powder with a slight alkaline taste. Has culinary and medicinal uses.

Borax: a mineral hydrated sodium tetrabate found on alkaline lake shores. Has medicinal and cosmetic uses.

Buttermilk: the milk which remains after butter has been separated from cream by churning. Used in home-cheesemaking and cosmetics.

Calamus Root: the root of a reed-like plant used as an aromatic fixative in scents and fragrances. Also has culinary uses.

Camomile: a daisy-like herb with culinary, cosmetic and medicinal uses.

Cardamom: a perennial shrub which grows abundantly on the Malabar Coast up in the Cardamom Hills. After flowering, pods are produced which contain the seeds. (Always buy the pods and grind the seeds yourself.)

Cassia bark: from a tropical tree, native of China. The aroma is similar to cinnamon but stronger. Used as an aromatic fixative in fragrances and scents; also has culinary uses.

Caustic soda: sodium hydroxide, one of the three main ingredients of soap. The liquid used for steeping certain wood ashes is evaporated to a powder form.

Cedarwood oil: extracted from the wood of several species of coniferous cedar tree. Used in cosmetics and fragrances.

Celery seed: seeds of the vegetable celery which originally grew wild on the European salt marshes. The seeds are more pungent than the plant.

Charcoal: carbon residue of charred wood etc. Instant burning charcoal is chemically treated.

Chili: member of the pepper family but much hotter than the capsicum. Basis for many Latin American, Indian and West Indian dishes.

Chocolate Vermicelli: vermicelli is a very slender macaroni. The chocolate variety is used to garnish sweets and cakes, etc.

Cinnamon: the dried inner bark of ' ' cinnamon tree which grows mainly Lanka and India. Has culinary ‚

---

medicinal uses.

Civit oil: extracted from a substance found in the anal sacs of the civit cat. Used as an aromatic fixative in fragrances and perfumes*.

Cloves: dried flower buds of the clove tree, a member of the myrtle family, native of the Moluccas Islands. A highly aromatic oil is extracted from cloves. Has culinary and medicinal uses, also used in fragrances.

Cocoa butter: solidified waxy oil from roasted cocoa beans. Has culinary and cosmetic uses.

Comphrey: a perennial herb, native of temperate Europe and Asia. Has culinary, cosmetic and medicinal uses.

Coriander: an annual which is cultivated throughout temperate regions of the world. The dried fruit (or seed) has culinary and medicinal uses. The oil extracted from the seed is used in some perfumes.

Corn meal: ground corn, used as a rough bread-making flour; also used in cosmetics.

Crab apples: small wild apples, usually bright yellow. Ideal for jelly-making.

Cream of tartar: odourless, colourless crystals or white crystalline powder with a pleasant acid taste. Has culinary and medicinal uses.

Desiccated coconut: small flakes of coconut preserved by drying and shredded to various thicknesses.

Elderflowers: tiny cream flowers of the elder tree which grows wild in most temperate regions. The flowers and berries have culinary, medicinal and cosmetic uses.

Emulsifying wax: made from ceto stearyl alcohol and sodium lauryl sulphate. Used as a stabilizer in cosmetic creams.

Essential oil: oils forming the odorous principles of fragrant flowers, herbs and barks, etc.

Fennel: a perennial herb, native of Southern Europe, commonly used a a vegetable. The flavour of fennel seeds is similar to aniseeds.

Fixative: gum benzoin, orris root powder etc., these are added to pot-pourris, pomanders or herb bags in order to hold or fix their fragrances.

Flour: *Buckwheat* is a polonum of the knotgrass family, having swollen joints and sheathing stipules. Used as cattle or fowl feed in Europe, but made into delicious breakfast cakes in U.S.A. *Cornflour* a nonwheat flour unsuitable for bread-making on its own because of lack of gluten. It makes an excellent thickening agent. *Strong Plain* is a bleached flour made from strong or 'hard' wheat which grows in extreme climates, Canada and Russia, and has a high gluten content. *Plain* flour is also bleached. It is a mixture of strong and 'soft' flours. The soft flour comes from wheat grown in temperate climates, Great Britain and parts of Australia. This flour is more suitable for cakes and short pastries. *Wholewheat* or wholemeal (the same flour with variations in the coarseness of the grinding) contains the whole of the wheat grain — the germ, the endosperm (starch) and the bran (outer layers). *Wheatmeal* contains 80–90 per cent wholewheat and consequently has a lighter texture than 100 per cent wholewheat.

Frangipani oil: used in perfumes, extracted from the red jasmine and similar species of the tropical American shrub.

Frankincense: one of the main ingredients of incense. It is a resin taken from the Boswellia tree which grows in Somalia and parts of Arabia.

Fuller's earth: a mineral-rich clay which absorbs oils. Used in cosmetics.

Garlic: a perennial, and member of the lily family. It has culinary and medicinal uses. A clove of garlic is one segment of the whole bulb.

Gelatine powder: odourless and tasteless glue extracted from bones and hides. Has culinary and cosmetic uses.

Germination: the point at which the seed of a plant begins to grow, to send out roots and stem.

Ginger: the rhizome or underground stem of ginger, a tropical perennial plant. Has culinary and medicinal uses. *Root* or *Stem ginger* is the underground stem, partially dried in the sun. *Ground ginger* is the stem ground to a fine powder and used in curries, cakes etc. *Preserved* or *candied* is the ginger root boiled and preserved in a strong sugar solution. *Crystallised ginger* has been removed from the sugar solution, washed, drained then dipped in caster sugar.

Glycerine: a colourless, neutral, odourless liquid, with a sweet taste, which attracts and holds moisture. Used in cosmetics and medicines.

Gum Arabic: resin extracted from acacia plants. Sold in powder form and used as a fixative in perfumes and cosmetics; also has culinary uses.

Gum benzoin: resin extracted from the benzoin tree of Java and Sumatra. Bought in rock form and ground to a powder with pestle or fingers. Tincture of benzoin is the liquid form. Used as a fixative in cosmetics and perfumes.

Hops: flowers of the hop plant, of the mulberry family, which has long twining stalks. Used to flavour beer, also used in some medicines and included in herb pillows for the induction of sleep.

Hybrid: a plant produced by cross-breeding two plants of different species or genera.

Kaolin: fine, white china clay used as an absorbing agent in cosmetics.

Lanolin (hydrous): the thick sticky fat from sheep's wool which has added water and is therefore lighter and smoother than anhydrous lanolin. Used in cosmetics.

Lard: fat rendered from pork, used in cooking and soap-making.

Lavender: a perennial shrub used as a basis for many perfumes and cosmetics. Native of mountainous regions of Mediterranean. Essential oil is extracted from the blossoms.

Lemon grass oil: extracted from certain perennial grasses of India. Used in perfumes and cosmetics.

Lemon verbena: a deciduous herb (shrub) native of tropical regions. Has culinary and medicinal uses.

Liquid glucose (corn syrup): colourless, odourles, very viscous syrup with a sweet taste. It consists of a mixture of dextrose, maltrose, dextrims and water. Has culinary and medicinal uses.

Liquid paraffin: a mixture of liquid hydrocarbons varying in composition according to the source of the petroleum from which it is obtained. It is a transparent, colourless, odourless and tasteless oily liquid, with medicinal and cosmetic uses.

Mace: the fruit of the nutmeg tree, native of the Moluccas and other East Indian islands, is similar to an apricot. When ripe it splits open to reveal the kernel or seed — the nutmeg — which is wrapped in blades of mace. The nutmeg and mace are separated and dried for commercial use.

Mustard: annual plant with clusters of

bright yellow flowers, grown throughout temperate regions of the world. The two main varieties produce a black seed or a creamy white seed. The black is more pungent. Mustard powder is a mixture of black and white seeds with turmeric or saffron added for colour.

Musk oil: extracted from the sexual secretions of the male musk deer. Used as an aromatic fixative in fragrances, also as a basis for perfumes.*

Nutmeg: see Mace. Both nutmeg and mace have culinary and medicinal uses.

Oatmeal: ground oats, the texture determined by the level of grinding. Has culinary and cosmetic uses. Often mixed with a wheat flour for bread-making because of its low gluten content.

Olive oil: extracted from the small fruits of the olive tree, grows in Mediterranean areas. Has culinary and cosmetic uses. A heavier low-grade oil is extracted from the olive stones and used in soap and candle making.

Orange flower oil (Neroli oil): distilled from orange blossoms, the white flowers of the citrus orange tree which grows in sub-tropical regions. Used in cosmetics and perfumes.

Orange flower water: a solution of oil of Neroli (see Orange flower oil). Has cosmetic and medicinal uses.

Orange oil: extracted from the rind of oranges.

Paraffin wax: mixture of solid hydrocarbons obtained by distillation from petroleum or from oil produced in the distillation of shale. Has medicinal and cosmetic uses.

Pasteurization: the partial sterilization of milk by heating it to 160°F (71°C) for 15 seconds and cooling it rapidly.

Pearl barley: barley grain stripped of the husk and pellicle (film of skin) and rounded by grinding. A decoction of pearl barley is the basic ingredient of lemon barley water.

Pectin: a mixture of carbohydrates found in the cell walls of fruits — important for the setting of jellies. Also has medicinal uses.

Pepper (capsicum): a sweet, bell-shaped vegetable. Green and red capsicums are of the same variety — the green is less ripe and will eventually turn red. Yellow or white capsicums are of a different variety. All can be eaten raw or cooked.

Pepper: berries of the perennial vine, native of the Malabar Coast. *Black peppercorns* are the unripe berries, harvested when they are green, then left to dry in the sun. *Green peppercorns* are the same unripe berries, usually pickled in brine to retain their softness. *White peppercorns* are the ripened berries with the black outer husk removed. *Cayenne pepper* is made from dried ground chillies. *Paprika pepper* is made from dried red capsicums.

Peppermint oil: is present in all parts of the peppermint plant (one of several varieties of the family Labiatae) which contains a high content of menthol. The oil is distilled and used to flavour liqueurs, confectionary, toothpaste, medicines, etc.

Purée: food reduced to a pulp and usually passed through a sieve or liquidizer.

Quince: the yellow fruit of an apple-like tree which ripens in Britain in September/October, and often grows wild along hedge-rows. The fruit is a bumpy, irregular pear shape and is used for jams etc.

Rennet: a substance containing rennin which is found in the stomach of young mammals — calves or kids — and curdles the milk without souring it.

Rose hips: the fruit or berries which are left after the flowers of the Dog rose, Wild rose or Sweet briar have wilted. Rose hip syrup and purée are rich in vitamin C.

Rosemary: a fragrant perennial shrub with succulent leaves like pine needles. Native of Mediterranean areas. Has culinary, cosmetic and medicinal uses.

Rose water: distilled from highly fragrant rose petals. Has culinary and cosmetic uses.

Sage: a hardy perennial which grows wild in Southern Europe. Has extensive culinary, cosmetic and medicinal uses.

Salt: chloride of sodium, occuring naturally as a mineral (rock-salt) and in solution in sea water, brine springs etc. *Table salt* is fine ground, free flowing salt and contains magnesium carbonate. *Cooking salt* is not so finely ground. *Sea* or *Kosher salt* contains natural iodine and other minerals. This is often sprinkled on meats prior to serving, or on breads just before baking. *Vegetable salt* is sodium chloride with added vegetable extracts — celery, onion, garlic salt.

Sandalwood: the highly fragrant wood of a parasitic tree of the East Indies. An essential oil is extracted from the wood. Used in cosmetics and fragrances.

Sesame seeds: from the tall annual, native of tropical climates. After threshing, the seeds are cleaned, dried and hulled. They have culi-nary uses. A polyunsaturated oil is extracted from the seeds and has culinary and cosmetic uses.

Seville orange: a bitter tasting orange if eaten in the normal way. Excellent for marmalades. Used extensively in Spain and Greece to make fish sauces.

Starter: the replacement (in cheese-making) of certain bacteria which were destroyed by pasteurization and which are needed to form lactic acid.

Stearic acid: a fatty acid used in candle making. It hardens the wax and makes it receptive to colour.

Sterilization: the destruction of micro-organisms by boiling for twenty minutes or using a sterilizing solution.

Sunflower oil: all parts of the sunflower, native of Central America, can be used. The first oil pressing, extracted from the seeds, has culinary uses. Subsequent pressings are used for soaps, candles and as poultry and cattle fodder.

Thyme: a hardy perennial, native of Mediterranean regions, with a strong, slightly sharp flavour. Has culinary and medicinal uses.

Tincture of myrrh: the liquid form of an aromatic transparent gum exuded from the bark of the commiphora tree, native of tropical Africa and Asia. Used as a fixative in cosmetics and fragrances.

Tragacanth: a gum resin extracted from thorny shrubs of the astagalus family. Bought in powder or ribbon form. Used as an aromatic fixative in fragrances.

Turkey Red oil: caster oil which has been treated so that it will disperse when added to water.

Turmeric: a bright yellow spice from the underground rhizome of the plant (as ginger), cultivated in India and China. Has culinary uses. Also used as a cloth dye. An essential oil, curcuma, is extracted from the roots and used in some perfumes.

Vanilla essence: this is often a synthetic substance which lacks the delicate flavour of true vanilla. Vanilla extract should be asked for. The vanilla pod, which contains the flavour, is the fruit of the orchid vine, native of Central America.

Vinegar: sour wine — a natural process in which alcohol is turned into acetic acid. *Wine vinegar*, red or white, is made from wine and will not dominate in culinary dishes. *Malt vinegar*, made from beer, has a powerful flavour and should only be used for pickling and chutney-making. *Cider vinegar*, made from cider, has a distinct flavour and should only be used where recipes specify it. *Distilled vinegar* is colourless and has a higher acetic acid content. It is excellent for preserving. Vinegar also has cosmetic and medicinal uses.

Vitamin E capsules: contain wheatgerm oil with extra vitamin E added. They are used in medicines and cosmetics.

Vodka: a spirit distilled from rye. Used as a preservative or an astringent in cosmetics.

Witch Hazel: distilled from the bark of the hamamelis or elder shrub. Used in cosmetics.

Woodruff: a low carpeting perennial, grows wild in temperate regions, usually found in woods. Odourless when fresh but smells like new-mown hay when dried. Has culinary uses, also used in fragrances.

Yeast: a substance consisting of minute fungi which produce zymase and induce the fermentation of carbohydrates. There are two kinds available for bread-making; fresh or dried (granular). The fresh can be bought from some bakers or supermarkets, the dried is packeted and sold at most groceries or supermarkets. (See chapter on bread-making.)

Ylang-ylang oil: extracted from the flowers of the ylang-ylang tree of the Philippines and parts of Malaya. Used in perfumes.

*In the interests of wildlife conservation, it is much better to buy one of the concentrated artificial essences which are just as potent and far less expensive.

U.S. Equivalents

Bicarbonate of soda	— Baking soda
Black treacle	— Molasses
Caster sugar	— Fine sugar
Caustic soda	— Commercial lye
Cornflower	— Corn starch
Dessicated coconut	— Shredded coconut
Digestive biscuit	— Graham cracker
Double cream	— Heavy cream
Fresh yeast	— Compressed yeast
Gelatine	— Gelatin
Icing sugar	— Confectioners' sugar
Liquid glucose	— Corn syrup
Minced beef	— Ground beef
Single cream	— Light cream
Strong plain flour	— Bread flour (high gluten content)
Sultana	— Raisin
Sweet	— Candy
Tomato chutney	— Chili sauce
Vanilla essence	— Vanilla extract
Wholewheat flour	— Whole grain or Graham flour

Index